松涛館流空手道形教範全集
KATA GUIDE BOOK FOR ALL JAPAN KARATEDO SHOTOKAN

基本形 KIHON KATA
平安初段～五段・鉄騎初段

平安初段
Heian Shodan

平安二段
Heian Nidan

平安三段
Heian Sandan

平安四段
Heian Yondan

平安五段
Heian Godan

鉄騎初段
Tekki Shodan

一般財団法人全日本空手道松涛館

もくじ
contents

平安初段　Heian Shodan ・・・・・・・・・・・ 5
　全挙動紹介　・・・・・・・・・・・・・・・ 6
　各挙動解説　・・・・・・・・・・・・・・・ 10

平安二段　Heian Nidan ・・・・・・・・・・・ 23
　全挙動紹介　・・・・・・・・・・・・・・・ 24
　各挙動解説　・・・・・・・・・・・・・・・ 28

平安三段　Heian Sandan ・・・・・・・・・・・ 41
　全挙動紹介　・・・・・・・・・・・・・・・ 42
　各挙動解説　・・・・・・・・・・・・・・・ 46

平安四段　Heian Yondan ・・・・・・・・・・・ 59
　全挙動紹介　・・・・・・・・・・・・・・・ 60
　各挙動解説　・・・・・・・・・・・・・・・ 64

平安五段　Heian Godan ・・・・・・・・・・・ 77
　全挙動紹介　・・・・・・・・・・・・・・・ 78
　各挙動解説　・・・・・・・・・・・・・・・ 82

鉄騎初段　Tekki Shodan ・・・・・・・・・・・ 93
　全挙動紹介　・・・・・・・・・・・・・・・ 94
　各挙動解説　・・・・・・・・・・・・・・・ 98

（一財）全日本空手道松涛館の成立

■ 2014年6月6日
「一般財団法人全日本空手道松涛館」を設立・登記

■ 2014年6月7日
公益財団法人全日本空手道連盟の評議員会において協力団体として承認

■ 2014年9月22日
（一財）全日本空手道松涛館設立記念祝賀会開催
（於　東京都・浅草ビューホテル）

■ 2015年7月12日
（一財）全日本空手道松涛館第1回全国空手道選手権大会開催
（於　東京都・日本武道館）

■ 2015年12月27日
全9地区協議会設立完了

■ 2016年4月
（一財）全日本空手道松涛館『松涛館流空手道形教範全集　基本形』発刊

平安初段
Heian Shodan
(21 挙動)

基本となる技である順突き、下段払い、揚（あげ）受け、手刀受けで構成されている。立ち方は前屈立ち、後屈立ちの2つだけである。この形ではすり足での運足や軸足のつくりや方向転換などを体得する。平安形の中ではもっとも基本的な技が含まれているので、絶えず繰り返し行ない、これを習熟することがこれからの形を学ぶ土台をつくることになる。特殊な使い方としては相手に手首をつかまれたときの拳槌（けんつい）縦回し打ちがある。演武線はほぼ「工」字形になる。

The basic (*kihon*) techniques included in Heian Shodan are Junzuki (punch), Gedan-Barai (low sweeping block), Age-Uke (rising block), and Shuto-Uke (knife hand block). There are only two stances, which are Zenkutsudachi and Kokutsudachi. This kata will help you become proficient in the Suri-Ashi (sliding foot) movement of keeping a center of balance on one foot, while moving the other, and even changing directions with it. As this kata contains the most elementary techniques of the Heian series many moves are repeated. This repetition is a cornerstone of learning and familiarising oneself with all kata. A special use of this kata is learning to strike with Tate-Mawashi-Uchi (hammer fist) when your wrist is grabbed by an opponent. The 'footprint' movement line for Heian Shodan looks similar to a capital 'I'.

平安初段　挙動一覧

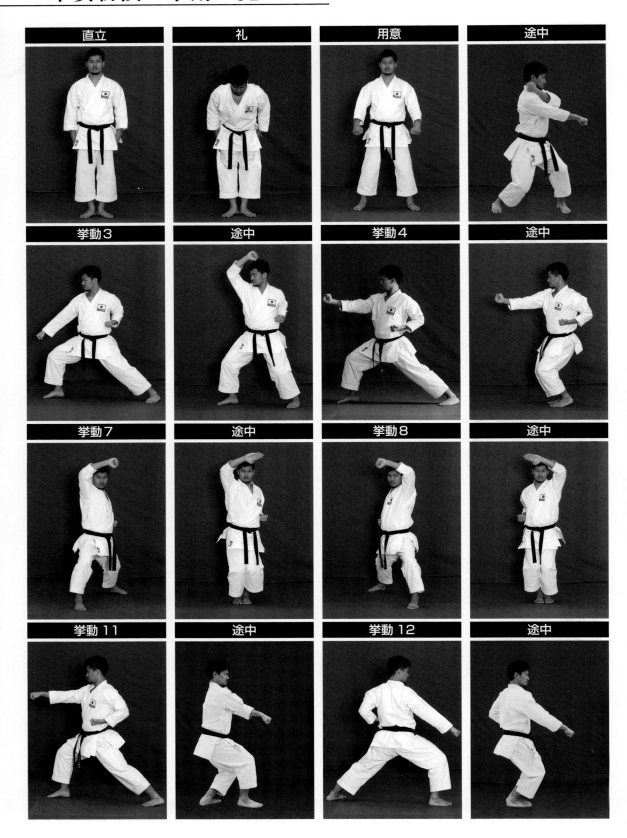

平安初段　各挙動解説

① 直立

② 礼

③ 用意

④ 途中

【手の動作】
両手は開いて大腿部両側につけて伸ばす

【足の動作】
結び立ち（左右とも正面に対して約30度）

※礼をする

【手の動作】
両拳を大腿部前にもっていく

【足の動作】
左足、右足の順に開いて八字立ち

【手の動作】
左拳は右肩上、右拳は左ななめ下に出し、次の動作の準備

【足の動作】
右脚を軸に体を左に回転させ、左足をすり足で進める

【Hands】
Open both hands and stretch the arms down to the sides of the thighs.

【Feet】
Musubidachi (left and right feet are angled approximately 30 degrees from front).

※ Bow (Rei).

【Hands】
Move both fists to in front of the thighs.

【Feet】
In order, move left foot then right foot to Hachijidachi.

【Hands】
Prepare for the next move by moving left fist to right shoulder and crossing the right arm diagonally down in front of the left hip.

【Feet】
Using the right foot as a pivot rotate to the left, move the left foot forward using Suri-Ashi.

挙動1	途中	挙動2	途中
 ⑤	 ⑥	 ⑦	 ⑧

【手の動作】
左下段払い
左拳を左膝上拳2つ程度あける

【足の動作】
左前屈立ち

※半身

【手の動作】
手はそのまま

【足の動作】
左脚を軸に右足をすり足で前に進める

【手の動作】
右中段順突き

【足の動作】
右前屈立ち

【手の動作】
右拳は左肩上、左拳は右ななめ下に出し、次の動作の準備

【足の動作】
左脚を軸に体を右に回転させ、右足を反対方向に移動し、すり足で前に進める

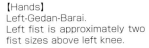

【Hands】
Left-Gedan-Barai.
Left fist is approximately two fist sizes above left knee.

【Feet】
Left-Zenkutsudachi.

※ Body is half turned (Hanmi).

【Hands】
Keep hands in the same position.

【Feet】
Pivoting on the left foot, move the right foot forward using Suri-Ashi.

【Hands】
Right-Chudan-Junzuki.

【Feet】
Right-Zenkutsudachi.

【Hands】
Prepare for the next move by moving the right fist to left shoulder and crossing the left arm diagonally down in front of the right hip.

【Feet】
Using the left foot as a pivot rotate to the right, and pull the right foot to face the opposite direction using Suri-Ashi.

挙動3 / 途中 / 挙動4 / 途中

⑨　⑩　⑪　⑫

【手の動作】
右下段払い

【足の動作】
右前屈立ち

※半身

【手の動作】
右拳は肩を中心に額の前を回し、次の動作の準備

【足の動作】
右足を半歩引き寄せる

【手の動作】
右拳槌縦回し打ち
（右拳は肩の高さ）

【足の動作】
引き寄せた右足をもとの位置に戻し、右前屈立ち

※半身

【手の動作】
手はそのまま

【足の動作】
右脚を軸に左足をすり足で前に進める

【Hands】
Right-Gedan-Barai.

【Feet】
Right-Zenkutsudachi.

※ Body is half turned (Hanmi).

【Hands】
Using the shoulder as centre, draw the right fist to infront of the forehead in a circular motion, in preparation for the next movement.

【Feet】
Draw the right foot half a step back.

【Hands】
Right-Kentsui-Tate-Mawashi-Uchi.
(Right fist is shoulder height.)

【Feet】
Return the right foot back to its original position, Right-Zenkutsudachi.

※ Body is half turned (Hanmi).

【Hands】
Keep hands in the same position.

【Feet】
Pivoting on the right foot, move the left foot forward using Suri-Ashi.

挙動3～4の解釈

◀ つかまれた右手首をはずすため、右足を半歩引き寄せると同時に右手首を引き、右足をもとにもどすと同時に拳槌で相手の鎖骨を打つ。

Simultaneously draw in the right foot half a step and pull the right wrist away to break the opponent's grip, then return the right foot to its original position, striking with a hammerfist(Kentsui) down onto the collarbone at the same time.

挙動5	途中	挙動6	途中
 ⑬	 ⑭	 ⑮	 ⑯

【手の動作】
左中段順突き

【足の動作】
左前屈立ち

【手の動作】
左拳は右肩上、右拳は左ななめ下に出し、次の動作の準備

【足の動作】
右脚を軸に体を左に回転させて、左足を正面に移動させる

【手の動作】
左下段払い

【足の動作】
左前屈立ち

※半身

【手の動作】
左拳を開き、左前腕を額前にあげる

【足の動作】
左脚を軸に右足をすり足で前に進める

【Hands】
Left-Chudan-Junzuki.

【Feet】
Left-Zenkutsudachi.

【Hands】
Prepare for the next move by moving left fist to right shoulder and crossing the right arm diagonally down in front of the left hip.

【Feet】
Using the right foot as a pivot rotate to the left, and pull the left foot to face the front using Suri-Ashi.

【Hands】
Left-Gedan-Barai.

【Feet】
Left-Zenkutsudachi.

※ Body is half turned (Hanmi).

【Hands】
Open the left fist and raise the left forearm to infront of the forehead.

【Feet】
Pivoting on the left foot, move the right foot forward using Suri-Ash`.

13

| 挙動7 | 途中 | 挙動8 | 途中 |

⑰　⑱　⑲　⑳

【手の動作】
右上段揚受け
額から拳1つ程度あける

【足の動作】
右前屈立ち

※半身

【手の動作】
右拳を開く

【足の動作】
右脚を軸に左足をすり足で前に進める

【手の動作】
左上段揚受け

【足の動作】
左前屈立ち

※半身

【手の動作】
左拳を開く

【足の動作】
左脚を軸に右足をすり足で前に進める

【Hands】
Right-Jodan-Age-Uke.
Held about one fist size in front of the forehead.

【Feet】
Right-Zenkutsudachi.

※ Body is half turned (Hanmi).

【Hands】
Open the right fist.

【Feet】
Pivoting on the right foot, move the left foot forward using Suri-Ashi.

【Hands】
Left-Jodan-Age-Uke.

【Feet】
Left-Zenkutsudachi.

※ Body is half turned (Hanmi).

【Hands】
Open the left fist.

【Feet】
Pivoting on the left foot, move the right foot forward using Suri-Ashi.

挙動9

途中

挙動10

途中

【手の動作】
右上段揚受け

【足の動作】
右前屈立ち

【留意点】
気合いを入れる

※半身

【手の動作】
左拳は右肩上、右拳は左ななめ下に出し、次の動作の準備

【足の動作】
右脚を軸に体を左に回転し、左足を移動させ、すり足で前に進める

【手の動作】
左下段払い

【足の動作】
左前屈立ち

※半身

【手の動作】
手はそのまま

【足の動作】
左脚を軸に右足をすり足で前に進める

【Hands】
Right-Jodan-Age-Uke.

【Feet】
Right-Zenkutsudachi.

【Note】
Kiai point.

※ Body is half turned (Hanmi).

【Hands】
Prepare for the next move by moving left fist to right shoulder and crossing the right arm diagonally down in front of the left hip.

【Feet】
Using the right foot as a pivot rotate counter-clockwise, and pull the left foot using Suri-Ashi.

【Hands】
Left-Gedan-Barai.

【Feet】
Left-Zenkutsudachi.

※ Body is half turned (Hanmi).

【Hands】
Keep hands in the same position.

【Feet】
Pivoting on the left foot, move the right foot forward using Suri-Ashi.

挙動11

挙動12

【手の動作】
右中段順突き

【足の動作】
右前屈立ち

【手の動作】
右拳は左肩上、左拳は右ななめ下に出し、次の動作の準備

【足の動作】
左脚を軸に体を右に回転させ、右足を反対方向に移動し、すり足で前に進める

【手の動作】
右下段払い

【足の動作】
右前屈立ち
※半身

【手の動作】
手はそのまま

【足の動作】
右脚を軸に左足をすり足で前に進める

【Hands】
Right-Chudan-Junzuki.

【Feet】
Right-Zenkutsudachi.

【Hands】
Prepare for the next move by moving right fist to left shoulder and crossing the left arm diagonally down in front of the right hip.

【Feet】
Using the left foot as a pivot rotate to the right, and pull the right foot to face the opposite direction using Suri-Ashi.

【Hands】
Right-Gedan-Barai.

【Feet】
Right-Zenkutsudachi.

※ Body is half turned (Hanmi).

【Hands】
Keep hands in the same position.

【Feet】
Pivoting on the right foot, move the left foot forward using Suri-Ashi.

挙動13

㉙

㉚ 途中

挙動14

㉛

㉜ 途中

後ろ

後ろ

後ろ

【手の動作】
左中段順突き

【足の動作】
左前屈立ち

【手の動作】
左拳は右肩上、右拳は左ななめ下に出し、次の動作の準備

【足の動作】
右脚を軸に体を左に回転し、左足を裏正面に移動させる

【手の動作】
左下段払い

【足の動作】
左前屈立ち

※半身

【手の動作】
手はそのまま

【足の動作】
左脚を軸に右足をすり足で前に進める

【Hands】
Left-Chudan-Junzuki.

【Feet】
Left-Zenkutsudachi.

【Hands】
Prepare for the next move by moving left fist to right shoulder and crossing the right arm diagonally down in front of the left hip.

【Feet】
Using the right foot as a pivot rotate to the left, and pull the left foot to face the rear using Suri-Ashi.

【Hands】
Left-Gedan-Barai.

【Feet】
Left-Zenkutsudachi.

※ Body is half turned (Hanmi).

【Hands】
Keep hands in the same position.

【Feet】
Pivoting on the left foot, move the right foot forward using Suri-Ashi.

挙動 15	途中	挙動 16	途中

【手の動作】
右中段順突き

【足の動作】
右前屈立ち

【手の動作】
手はそのまま

【足の動作】
右脚を軸に左足をすり足で前に進める

【手の動作】
左中段順突き

【足の動作】
左前屈立ち

【手の動作】
手はそのまま

【足の動作】
左脚を軸に右足をすり足で前に進める

【Hands】
Right-Chudan-Junzuki.

【Feet】
Right-Zenkutsudachi.

【Hands】
Keep hands in the same position.

【Feet】
Pivoting on the right foot, move the left foot forward using Suri-Ashi.

【Hands】
Left-Chudan-Junzuki.

【Feet】
Left-Zenkutsudachi.

【Hands】
Keep hands in the same position.

【Feet】
Pivoting on the left foot, move the right foot forward using Suri-Ashi.

挙動 17

【手の動作】
右中段順突き

【足の動作】
右前屈立ち

【留意点】
気合いを入れる

【Hands】
Right-Chudan-Junzuki.

【Feet】
Right-Zenkutsudachi.

【Note】
Kiai point.

途中

【手の動作】
左掌は右肩上、右掌は甲を上にしてやや左ななめ下に出し、次の動作の準備

【足の動作】
右脚を軸に体を左に回転し、左足を移動させ、すり足で前に進める

【Hands】
Prepare for the next move by positioning the left open palm above the right shoulder. With the back of the hand facing up, extend the right open palm out in front, pointing slightly diagonally downward.

【Feet】
Using the right foot as a pivot rotate counter-clockwise, and pull the left foot using Suri-Ashi.

挙動 18

【手の動作】
左手刀中段受け

【足の動作】
右後屈立ち

【Hands】
Left-Chudan-Shuto-Uke.

【Feet】
Right-Kokutsudachi.

途中

【手の動作】
右掌は左肩上、左掌は甲を上にしてやや右ななめ下に出し、次の動作の準備

【足の動作】
左脚を軸に右足をすり足で斜め前に進める

【Hands】
Prepare for the next move by positioning the right open palm above the left shoulder. With the back of the hand facing up, extend the left open palm out in front, pointing slightly diagonally downward.

【Feet】
Pivoting on the left foot, move the right foot diagonally forward using Suri-Ashi.

後ろ

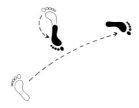

挙動 19 / 途中 / 挙動 20 / 途中

【手の動作】
右手刀中段受け

【足の動作】
左後屈立ち

【手の動作】
右掌は左肩上、左掌は甲を上にしてやや右ななめ下に出し、次の動作の準備

【足の動作】
左脚を軸に体を右に回転させ、右に右足を移動し、すり足で前に進める

【手の動作】
右手刀中段受け

【足の動作】
左後屈立ち

【手の動作】
左掌は右肩上、右掌は甲を上にしてやや左ななめ下に出し、次の動作の準備

【足の動作】
右脚を軸に左足をすり足で斜め前に進める

【Hands】
Right-Chudan-Shuto-Uke.

【Feet】
Left-Kokutsudachi.

【Hands】
Prepare for the next move by positioning the right open palm above the left shoulder. With the back of the hand facing up, extend the left open palm out in front, pointing slightly diagonally downward.

【Feet】
Using the left foot as a pivot rotate to the right, and pull the right foot to face the right using Suri-Ashi.

【Hands】
Right-Chudan-Shuto-Uke.

【Feet】
Left-Kokutsudachi.

【Hands】
Prepare for the next move by positioning the left open palm above the right shoulder. With the back of the hand facing up, extend the right open palm out in front, pointing slightly diagonally downward.

【Feet】
Pivoting on the right foot, move the left foot diagonally forward using Suri-Ashi

挙動21	直れ	直立	礼

㊺	㊻	㊼	㊽

【手の動作】
左手刀中段受け

【足の動作】
右後屈立ち

【手の動作】
両拳を大腿部前にもっていく

【足の動作】
左足を引いて八字立ち

【手の動作】
両手は開いて大腿部両側につけて伸ばす

【足の動作】
左足、右足の順に閉じて結び立ち

※礼をする

【Hands】
Left-Chudan-Shuto-Uke.

【Feet】
Right-Kokutsudachi.

【Hands】
Move both fists to in front of the thighs.

【Feet】
Draw the left foot back into Hachijidachi.

【Hands】
Open both hands and stretch the arms down to the sides of the thighs.

【Feet】
In order, move left foot then right foot into Musubidachi.

※ Bow (Rei).

平安二段
Heian Nidan
（26 挙動）

手の動作に背腕側面上段受け、中段諸手受け、裏拳打ち、貫手、足の動作に横蹴り、前蹴りが加わり、ほとんどの基本技が含まれている形である。この形で突き、打ち、蹴りの技を体得することにより、空手道の基本技が一層広がる。特殊な使い方として逆半身になって技をかけることも体得する。演武線はほぼ「工」字形になる

Heian Nidan includes Haiwan-Sokumen-Jodan-Uke (blocking with the outside edge of the arm), Morote-Uke (reinforced block), Uraken-Uchi (back-fist strike), Nukite (spear-hand) for hand movements, as well as Yokogeri (side kick) and Maegeri (front kick) for foot movements. As such, this kata contains almost all 'kihon' techniques. As you comprehend the punching, striking and kicking techniques within this kata, the basic techniques of Karatedo are expanded upon much further. Special uses for this kata include becoming proficient in Gyaku-Hanmi position (the upper body is rotated in the opposite direction to the lower body). As with Heian Shodan, the 'footprint' movement line for Heian Nidan looks similar to a capital T.

平安二段　挙動一覧

平安二段　各挙動解説

① 直立

② 礼

③ 用意

④ 途中

【手の動作】
両手は開いて大腿部両側につけて伸ばす

【足の動作】
結び立ち（左右とも正面に対して約３０度）

※礼をする

【手の動作】
両拳を大腿部前にもっていく

【足の動作】
左足、右足の順に開いて八字立ち

【手の動作】
両拳そのままで、次の動作の準備

【足の動作】
右脚を軸に左足をすり足で進める

【Hands】
Open both hands and stretch the arms down to the sides of the thighs.

【Feet】
Musubidachi (left and right feet are angled approximately 30 degrees from front).

※ Bow (Rei).

【Hands】
Move both fists to in front of the thighs.

【Feet】
In order, move left foot then right foot to Hachijidachi.

【Hands】
Keeping both hands where they are, prepare for the next movement.

【Feet】
Pivot on the right foot and move the left foot forward using Suri-Ashi.

挙動１〜３の解釈

挙動1	挙動2	挙動3	途中

⑤	⑥	⑦	⑧

【手の動作】
左背腕左側面上段横受け、右前腕額前横構え
（左肘は左肩横、右前腕は額前にもっていく）

【足の動作】
右後屈立ち

【手の動作】
右拳槌左側面打込み、左手首流し受け
（左拳は右肩前に寄せ、右拳槌で左側面に打ち込む）

【足の動作】
立ち方はそのまま

【手の動作】
左拳左側面中段突き
右拳右腰

【足の動作】
立ち方はそのまま

【留意点】
挙動2〜3は続ける。

【手の動作】
両拳を左腰前に構える

【足の動作】
左脚を軸に体を右に回転する

【Hands】
Block Jodan-Yoko-Uke with the left arm to the left rear side, position the right forearm into Yoko-Kamae.
(The left elbow is level with the left shoulder, the right forearm is brought before the forehead.)

【Feet】
Right-Kokutsudachi.

【Hands】
Execute a Right-Kentsui-Uchikomi to the left side, and Nagashi-Uke with the left wrist.
(Bring the left fist in front of the right shoulder, and drive a right hammerfist to the left.)

【Feet】
Keep the same stance.

【Hands】
Execute a Left-Chudan-Tsuki to the left side.
Pull the right fist to the right hip.

【Feet】
Keep the same stance.

【Note】
Movements 2〜3 are continuous.

【Hands】
Position both fists in front of the left hip.

【Feet】
Using the left foot as a pivot rotate to the right.

◀左背腕で相手の上段突きを受け、続いて相手が左拳で上段を突いてきたとき、左手首で流し受けをしながら右拳槌で肘関節を打つ。続けて相手の中段を突く。

Block the opponent's Jodan-Tsuki with the outer edge of the left arm. When the opponent follows up with a Left-Jodan punch, while executing a Nagashi-Uke with the left wrist attack the elbow joint with a right hammerfist (Kentsui). Continue with a punch to the opponent's midsection.

29

挙動4	挙動5	挙動6	挙動7a
⑨	⑩	⑪	⑫

【手の動作】
右背腕右側面上段横受け、左前腕額前横構え
(右肘は右肩横、左前腕は額前にもっていく)

【足の動作】
左後屈立ち

【手の動作】
左拳槌右側面打込み、右手首流し受け
(右拳は左肩前に寄せ、左拳槌で右側面に打ち込む)

【足の動作】
立ち方はそのまま

【手の動作】
右拳右側面中段突き
左拳左腰

【足の動作】
立ち方はそのまま

【留意点】
挙動5〜6は続ける。

【手の動作】
右拳を左拳の上に重ねる

【足の動作】
左足を半歩寄せ、右足裏を左膝横につける

【Hands】
Block Jodan-Yoko-Uke with the right arm to the right rear side, position the left forearm into Yoko-Kamae.
(The right elbow is level with the right shoulder, the left forearm is brought before the forehead.)

【Feet】
Left-Kokutsudachi.

【Hands】
Execute a Left-Kentsui-Uchikomi to the Right side, and Nagashi-Uke with the right wrist.
(Bring the right fist in front of the left shoulder, and drive a left hammerfist to the right.)

【Feet】
Keep the same stance.

【Hands】
Execute a Right-Chudan-Tsuki to the right side.
Pull the left fist to the left hip.

【Feet】
Keep the same stance.

【Note】
Movements 5〜6 are continuous.

【Hands】
Place the right fist above the left fist.

【Feet】
Draw the left foot forward half a step, place the sole of the right foot next to the left knee.

挙動7b　途中　挙動8　途中

⑬　⑭　⑮　⑯

横

横

【手の動作】
右裏拳上段横回し打ち

【足の動作】
右足刀中段横蹴上げ
左脚立ち

【手の動作】
左掌は右肩上、右掌は甲を上にしてやや左ななめ下に出し、次の動作の準備

【足の動作】
膝をかい込む
立ち方はそのまま

【手の動作】
左手刀中段受け

【足の動作】
右後屈立ち

【手の動作】
右掌は左肩上、左掌は甲を上にしてやや右ななめ下に出し、次の動作の準備

【足の動作】
左脚を軸に右足をすり足で前に進める

 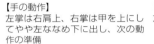  

【Hands】
Right-Uraken-Jodan-Yoko-Mawashi-Uchi.

【Feet】
Right-Sokuto-Chudan-Yoko-Keage.
Stand on left leg.

【Hands】
Prepare for the next move by positioning the left open palm above the right shoulder. With the back of the hand facing up, extend the right open palm out in front, pointing slightly diagonally downward.

【Feet】
Bring the knee back in front. Keep standing on the left leg.

【Hands】
Left-Chudan-Shuto-Uke.

【Feet】
Right-Kokutsudachi.

【Hands】
Prepare for the next move by positioning the right open palm above the left shoulder. With the back of the hand facing up, extend the left open palm out in front, pointing slightly diagonally downward.

【Feet】
Pivoting on the left foot, move the right foot forward using Suri-Ashi.

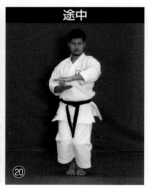

【手の動作】
右中段手刀受け

【足の動作】
左後屈立ち

【手の動作】
左掌は右肩上、右掌は甲を上にやや左ななめ下に出し、次の動作の準備

【足の動作】
右脚を軸に左足をすり足で前に進める

【手の動作】
左手刀中段受け

【足の動作】
右後屈立ち

【手の動作】
左腕は肘から先を胸前に倒す

【足の動作】
左脚を軸に右足をすり足で前に進める

【Hands】
Right-Chudan-Shuto-Uke.

【Feet】
Left-Kokutsudachi.

【Hands】
Prepare for the next move by positioning the left open palm above the right shoulder. With the back of the hand facing up, extend the right open palm out in front, pointing slightly diagonally downward..

【Feet】
Pivoting on the right foot, move the left foot forward using Suri-Ashi.

【Hands】
Left-Chudan-Shuto-Uke.

【Feet】
Right-Kokutsudachi.

【Hands】
From the elbow, bend the left arm down to in front of the chest.

【Feet】
Pivoting on the left foot, move the right foot forward using Suri-Ashi.

挙動 11

【手の動作】
右中段縦貫手（甲右向き）
左掌中段押さえ受け（甲上向き）

【足の動作】
右前屈立ち

【留意点】
気合いを入れる

【Hands】
Right-Chudan-Tate-Nukite (back of the hand facing right).
With the left hand, Chudan-Osae-Uke (back of the hand facing up).

【Feet】
Right-Zenkutsudachi.

【Note】
Kiai point.

途中

【手の動作】
左掌は右肩上、右掌は甲を上にしてやや左ななめ下に出し、次の動作の準備

【足の動作】
右脚を軸に体を左に回転し、左足を移動させ、すり足で前に進める

【Hands】
Prepare for the next move by positioning the left open palm above the right shoulder. With the back of the hand facing up, extend the right open palm out in front, pointing slightly diagonally downward.

【Feet】
Using the right foot as a pivot rotate counter-clockwise, and pull the left foot using Suri-Ashi.

挙動 12

【手の動作】
左手刀中段受け

【足の動作】
右後屈立ち

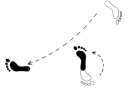

【Hands】
Left-Chudan-Shuto-Uke.

【Feet】
Right-Kokutsudachi.

途中

【手の動作】
右掌は左肩上、左掌は甲を上にしてやや右ななめ下に出し、次の動作の準備

【足の動作】
左脚を軸に右足をすり足で斜め前に進める

【Hands】
Prepare for the next move by positioning the right open palm above the left shoulder. With the back of the hand facing up, extend the left open palm out in front, pointing slightly diagonally downward.

【Feet】
Pivoting on the left foot, move the right foot diagonally forward using Suri-Ashi.

挙動 11 の解釈

◀ 左掌で相手の右手首を押さえながら水月に縦貫手をする。

While suppressing the opponent's right wrist with a left open hand, Attack the solaplexus with a Tate-Nukite.

挙動13	途中	挙動14	途中

㉕	㉖	㉗	㉘

【手の動作】
右手刀中段受け

【足の動作】
左後屈立ち

【手の動作】
右掌は左肩上、左掌は甲を上にしてやや右ななめ下に出し、次の動作の準備

【足の動作】
左脚を軸に体を右に回転し、右足を移動させ、すり足で前に進める

【手の動作】
右手刀中段受け

【足の動作】
左後屈立ち

【手の動作】
左掌は右肩上、右掌は甲を上にしてやや左ななめ下に出し、次の動作に備える

【足の動作】
右脚を軸に左足をすり足で斜め前に進める

【Hands】
Right-Chudan-Shuto-Uke.

【Feet】
Left-Kokutsudachi.

【Hands】
Prepare for the next move by positioning the right open palm above the left shoulder. With the back of the hand facing up, extend the left open palm out in front, pointing slightly diagonally downward.

【Feet】
Using the left foot as a pivot rotate to the right, move the right foot forward using Suri-Ashi.

【Hands】
Right-Chudan-Shuto-Uke.

【Feet】
Left-Kokutsudachi.

【Hands】
Prepare for the next move by positioning the left open palm above the right shoulder. With the back of the hand facing up, extend the right open palm out in front, pointing slightly diagonally downward.

【Feet】
Pivoting on the right foot, move the left foot forward using Suri-Ashi.

挙動15

㉙

【手の動作】
左手刀中段受け

【足の動作】
右後屈立ち

【Hands】
Left-Shuto-Chudan-Uke.

【Feet】
Right-Kokutsudachi.

途中

㉚

後ろ

【手の動作】
両掌を握り、両拳を交差させ、右拳を左肘の下にして、次の動作の準備

【足の動作】
右脚を軸に体を左に回転し左足を裏正面に移動させ、前屈立ちの半歩幅となる

【Hands】
Prepare for the next move by closing both fists and crossing them over, with the right fist moved to under the left elbow.

【Feet】
Pivoting on the right foot, move the left foot towards the rear using Suri-Ashi, to go into a half-length Zenkutsudachi.

挙動16

㉛

後ろ

【手の動作】
逆半身で右中段外受け

【足の動作】
左脚前屈（前屈立ちの半歩幅）

【Hands】
In reverse hanmi, Right-Chudan-Soto-Uke.

【Feet】
Left-Zenkutsu (half-stride length of Zenkutsudachi).

挙動17

㉜

後ろ

【手の動作】
手はそのまま

【足の動作】
右前蹴り
左脚立ち

【Hands】
Keep hands in the same position.

【Feet】
Right-Maegeri.
Stand on left leg.

35

挙動 18	途中	挙動 19	挙動 20

㉝	㉞	㉟	㊱
後ろ	 後ろ	 後ろ	 後ろ

【手の動作】
左拳中段逆突き

【足の動作】
右前屈立ち

【留意点】
挙動16〜18は続ける。

【手の動作】
両拳を交差し、左拳を右肘の下にして、次の動作の準備

【足の動作】
立ち方はそのまま

【手の動作】
逆半身で左中段外受け

【足の動作】
右脚前屈
（逆半身になり、右足を一足長引く）

【手の動作】
手はそのまま

【足の動作】
左前蹴り
右脚立ち

【Hands】
Left fist executes Chudan-Gyakuzuki.

【Feet】
Right-Zenkutsudachi.

【Note】
Movements 16 〜 18 are continuous.

【Hands】
Prepare for the next move by closing both fists and crossing them over, with the left fist moved to under the right elbow.

【Feet】
Keep the same stance.

【Hands】
In reverse hanmi, Left-Chudan-Soto-Uke.

【Feet】
Right-Zenkutsu.
(Pull the right foot one foot's length with body facing reverse hanmi)

【Hands】
Keep hands in the same position.

【Feet】
Left-Maegeri.
Stand on right leg.

挙動21

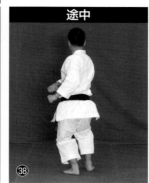
㊲ 後ろ

【手の動作】
右拳中段逆突き

【足の動作】
左前屈立ち

【留意点】
挙動19〜21は続ける。

【Hands】
Right fist executes Chudan-Gyakuzuki.

【Feet】
Left-Zenkutsudachi.

【Note】
Movements 19 〜 21 are continuous.

途中

㊳ 後ろ

【手の動作】
両拳を左腰前にもっていく

【足の動作】
左脚を軸にすり足で右足を前に進める

【Hands】
Bring both fists to in front of the left hip.

【Feet】
Pivoting on the left foot, move the right foot forward using Suri-Ashi.

挙動22

㊴ 後ろ

【手の動作】
右中段諸手受け
（右肘内側に左拳の小指側を添える）

【足の動作】
右前屈立ち

※半身

【Hands】
Right-Chudan-Morote-Uke (Align the little finger side of the left fist to the inside of the right elbow).

【Feet】
Right-Zenkutsudachi.

※ Body is half turned (Hanmi).

途中

㊵

【手の動作】
左拳は右肩上、右拳は左ななめ下に出し、次の動作の準備

【足の動作】
右脚を軸に体を左に回転させ左足を移動し、すり足で前に進める

【Hands】
Prepare for the next move by moving left fist to right shoulder and crossing the right arm diagonally down in front of the left hip.

【Feet】
Using the right foot as a pivot rotate counter-clockwise, and pull the left foot using Suri-Ashi.

37

挙動23	途中	挙動24	途中

㊶	㊷	㊸	㊹

【手の動作】
左下段払い

【足の動作】
左前屈立ち

※半身

【手の動作】
左拳を開いて額前にあげる

【足の動作】
左脚を軸に右足をすり足で斜め前に進める

【手の動作】
右上段揚受け

【足の動作】
右前屈立ち

※半身

【手の動作】
右拳は左肩上、左拳は右ななめ下に出し、次の動作の準備

【足の動作】
左脚を軸に体を右に回転させ右足を移動し、すり足で前に進める

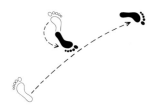

【Hands】
Left-Gedan-Barai.

【Feet】
Left-Zenkutsudachi.

※ Body is half turned.

【Hands】
Open the left fist and raise it to in front of the forehead.

【Feet】
Pivoting on the left foot, move the right foot diagonally forward using Suri-Ashi.

【Hands】
Right-Jodan-Age-Uke.

【Feet】
Right-Zenkutsudachi.

※ Body is half turned.

【Hands】
Prepare for the next move by moving the right fist to left shoulder and crossing the left arm diagonally down in front of the right hip.

【Feet】
Using the left foot as a pivot rotate the body to the right, move the right foot forward using Suri-Ashi.

挙動25	途中	挙動26	直れ

㊺	㊻	㊼	㊽

【手の動作】
右下段払い

【足の動作】
右前屈立ち

※半身

【手の動作】
右拳を開いて額前にあげる

【足の動作】
右脚を軸に左足をすり足で斜め前に進める

【手の動作】
左上段揚受け

【足の動作】
左前屈立ち

【留意点】
気合いを入れる

※半身

【手の動作】
両拳を大腿部前にもっていく

【足の動作】
左足を引いて八字立ち

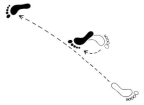  

【Hands】
Right-Gedan-Barai.

【Feet】
Right-Zenkutsudachi.

※ Body is half turned (Hanmi).

【Hands】
Open the right fist and raise it to in front of the forehead.

【Feet】
Pivoting on the right foot, move the left foot diagonally forward using Suri-Ashi.

【Hands】
Left-Jodan-Age-Uke.

【Feet】
Left-Zenkutsudachi.

【Note】
Kiai point.

※ Body is half turned.

【Hands】
Move both fists to in front of the thighs.

【Feet】
Draw the left foot back into Hachijidachi.

39

直立	礼

【手の動作】
両手は開いて大腿部両側につけて伸ばす

※礼をする

【足の動作】
左足、右足の順に閉じて結び立ち

【Hands】
Open both hands and stretch the arms down to the sides of the thighs.

※ Bow (Rei).

【Feet】
In order, move left foot then right foot into Musubidachi.

平安三段
Heian Sandan
（20 挙動）

手の動作に中段外受けと下段受けによる受け替え、肘受け、足の動作には騎馬立ちが加わる。騎馬立ちからの踏込み、寄り足など一段と高度な技の使い方を体得する。特殊な使い方として貫手の手首をつかまれ、ねじられたときの反撃、後方の相手に抱きつかれたときの肘と突きによる攻撃など多彩な技も体得できる。平安形の中では、騎馬立ちをもっとも多く使う。演武線は「T」字形になる。

Hand techniques in Heian Sandan include changing between Chudan-Soto-Uke (outer block) and Gedan-Uke (lower block) as well as Hiji-Uke (blocking with the elbow). Kibadachi is added to the foot movements. The use of advanced techniques such as Fumikomi (stamping), Yori-ashi (drawing the foot back) and so on from Kibadachi can also be understood from this kata. Special uses of Heian Sandan include becoming proficient in a variety of skills, such as countering when your Nukite hand is grabbed and twisted, as well as striking with both the elbow and fist when grabbed from behind. Kibadachi is used more here than in any other Heian kata. The 'footprint' movement line for this kata looks similar to a capital 'T'.

平安三段　挙動一覧

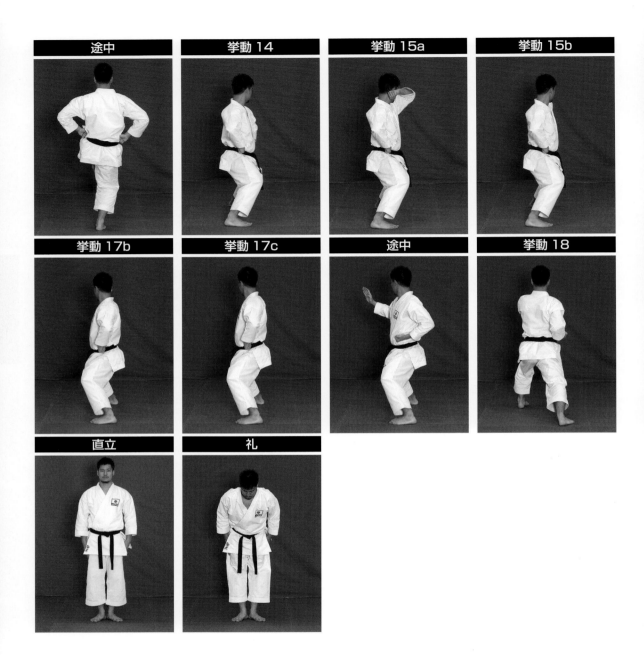

平安三段　各挙動解説

① 直立

② 礼

③ 用意

④ 途中

【手の動作】
両手は開いて大腿部両側につけて伸ばす

【足の動作】
結び立ち（左右とも正面に対して約30度）

※礼をする

【手の動作】
両拳を大腿部前にもっていく

【足の動作】
左足、右足の順に開いて八字立ち

【手の動作】
右拳は左横に出し、左拳は右腰前に持っていき、次の動作の準備

【足の動作】
右脚を軸に左足をすり足で進める

【Hands】
Open both hands and stretch the arms down to the sides of the thighs.

【Feet】
Musubidachi (left and right feet are angled approximately 30 degrees from front).

※ Bow (Rei).

【Hands】
Move both fists to in front of the thighs.

【Feet】
In order, move left foot then right foot to Hachijidachi.

【Hands】
Prepare for the next move by extending the right fist to the left side, while at the same time moving the left fist to in front of the right hip.

【Feet】
Using the right foot as a pivot rotate to the left, move the left foot forward using Suri-Ashi.

| 挙動1 | 途中 | 挙動2 | 途中 |

⑤

⑥

⑦

⑧

【手の動作】
左拳左側面中段外受け

【足の動作】
右後屈立ち

【手の動作】
右拳を左腰前から左手の外側を、左拳は右手の内側を回し、両腕を胸前で交差させながら、次の動作の準備

【足の動作】
左足はそのままにし、右足を引きつける

【手の動作】
右中段外受け、左下段受け

【足の動作】
閉足立ち

【手の動作】
右拳は左肩前から左手の内側を、左拳は右手の外側を回し、両腕を胸前で交差させながら、次の動作の準備

【足の動作】
立ち方はそのまま

【Hands】
To the left side, block Left-Chudan-Soto-Uke.

【Feet】
Right-Kokutsudachi.

【Hands】
Prepare for the next move by moving the right fist to in front of the left hip, then crossing the arms in front of the chest, keeping the left fist inside of the right hand.

【Feet】
Keeping the left foot in the same position, pull in the right foot.

【Hands】
Right-Chudan-Soto-Uke, Left-Gedan-Uke.

【Feet】
Heisokudachi.

【Hands】
Prepare for the next move by crossing both arms in front of the chest, rotating the right arm from in front of the left shoulder, and the right hand rotating on the inside of the left hand.

【Feet】
Keep the same stance.

47

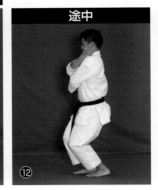

【手の動作】
左中段外受け、右下段受け

【足の動作】
立ち方はそのまま

【留意点】
挙動2〜3は続ける。

【手の動作】
右拳は左腰前に持っていき、左拳は右横に出し、次の動作の準備

【足の動作】
左脚を軸に体を右に回転し、右足をすり足で進める

【手の動作】
右中段外受け

【足の動作】
左後屈立ち

【手の動作】
右拳は左肩前から左手の内側を、左拳は右手の外側を回し、両拳を胸前で交差させながら、次の動作の準備

【足の動作】
右足はそのままにし、左足を引きつける

【Hands】
Left-Chudan-Soto-Uke, Right-Gedan-Uke.

【Feet】
Keep the same stance.

【Note】
Movements 2〜3 are continuous.

【Hands】
Prepare for the next move by extending the left fist to the right side, while at the same time moving the right fist to in front of the left hip.

【Feet】
Using the left foot as a pivot rotate clockwise, and pull the right foot using Suri-Ashi.

【Hands】
Right-Chudan-Soto-Uke.

【Feet】
Left-Kokutsudachi.

【Hands】
Prepare for the next move by crossing both arms in front of the chest, rotating the right arm from in front of the left shoulder, and the right hand rotating on the inside of the left hand.

【Feet】
Keeping the right foot in the same position, pull in the left foot.

48

【手の動作】
左中段外受け、右下段受け

【足の動作】
閉足立ち

【手の動作】
右拳は左手の外側を、左拳は右肩前から右手の内側を回し、両腕を胸前で交差させながら、次の動作の準備

【足の動作】
立ち方はそのまま

【手の動作】
右中段外受け、左下段受け

【足の動作】
立ち方はそのまま

【留意点】
挙動5～6は続ける。

【手の動作】
両拳を右腰前に持っていき、次の動作の準備

【足の動作】
顔を正面に向け、右脚を軸に左足を正面にすり足で進める

【Hands】
Left-Chudan-Soto-Uke, Right-Gedan-Uke.

【Feet】
Heisokudachi.

【Hands】
Prepare for the next move by crossing both arms in front of the chest, rotating the left arm from in front of the right shoulder, and the left hand rotating on the inside of the right hand.

【Feet】
Keep the same stance.

【Hands】
Right-Chudan-Soto-Uke, Left-Gedan-Uke.

【Feet】
Keep the same stance.

【Note】
Movements 5 ～ 6 are continuous.

【Hands】
Prepare for the next move by holding both fists in front of the right hip.

【Feet】
Turn your face to the front, and pivot on the right foot, moving the the left foot to the front using Suri-Ashi.

挙動7	途中	挙動8	途中
 ⑰	 ⑱	 ⑲	 ⑳

【手の動作】
左中段諸手受け（左肘内側に右拳の小指側を添える）

【足の動作】
右後屈立ち

【手の動作】
左拳は開掌し、肘を中心に倒し、右拳は開掌して次の動作の準備

【足の動作】
左脚を軸に右足をすり足で正面に進める

【手の動作】
右中段縦貫手（甲右向き）、左掌中段押え受け（甲上向き）

【足の動作】
右前屈立ち

【手の動作】
縦貫手の右掌を内側に捻りながら次の動作の準備

【足の動作】
立ち方はそのまま

【Hands】
Left-Chudan-Morote-Uke (Align the little finger side of the right fist to the inside of the left elbow).

【Feet】
Right-Kokutsudachi.

【Hands】
Prepare for the next move by opening the left hand, bending the arm down at the elbow, and opening the right hand.

【Feet】
Pivoting on the left foot, move the right foot to the front using Suri-Ashi.

【Hands】
Right-Chudan-Tate-Nukite (back of the hand facing right). With the left hand, Chudan-Osae-Uke (back of the hand facing up).

【Feet】
Right-Zenkutsudachi.

【Hands】
Prepare for the next move by twisting the right open hand to the inside.

【Feet】
Keep the same stance.

㉑ 途中 ／ ㉒ 途中 ／ ㉓ 挙動9 ／ ㉔ 途中

【手の動作】
右掌を右腰に引きつけながら、次の動作の準備

【足の動作】
右脚を軸に体を左に回転させる

【手の動作】
左拳は右肩前から次の動作の準備

【足の動作】
右脚を軸として、すり足で騎馬立ちの準備

【手の動作】
左拳槌中段横回打ち（右拳右腰）

【足の動作】
騎馬立ち

【手の動作】
手の位置はそのまま

【足の動作】
左脚を軸に右足を正面に進める

【Hands】
Prepare for the next move by pulling the right open hand to the right hip.

【Feet】
Using the right foot as a pivot rotate to the left.

【Hands】
Hold the left fist in front of the right shoulder, and prepare for the next move.

【Feet】
Pivoting on the right foot, prepare to move into Kibadachi using Suri-Ashi.

【Hands】
Left-Kentsui-Chudan-Yoko-Mawashi-Uchi (Pull the right fist to the right hip).

【Feet】
Kibadachi.

【Hands】
Keep hands in the same position.

【Feet】
Pivoting on the left foot, move the right foot to the front using Suri-Ashi.

挙動8〜9の解釈

◀右貫手の手首をつかまれてひねられたとき、相手にさからわずに体を回転させながら相手に近づき、左拳槌で中段（脇腹）を打つ。

Once the right wrist (Nukite hand) is grabbed and twisted, without resisting the opponent's grip rotate your body while drawing closer, and then strike with a left hammerfist (Kentsui) to the opponent's torso flank.

挙動 10

㉕

途中

㉖

挙動 11

㉗

途中

㉘

後ろ

後ろ

【手の動作】
右中段順突き

【足の動作】
右前屈立ち

【留意点】
気合いを入れる
挙動9〜10は続ける

【手の動作】
両拳を腰の位置に持っていく

【足の動作】
右脚を軸に体を左に回転させ、左足を右足に合わせ裏正面を向く

【手の動作】
両拳両腰構え（両甲前向き）

【足の動作】
閉足立ち

【留意点】
顔、手、足の動きを合わせ、ゆっくりと動かす

【手の動作】
手の位置はそのまま

【足の動作】
右膝を右胸にかい込む

【Hands】
Right-Chudan-Junzuki.

【Feet】
Right-Zenkutsudachi.

【Note】
Kiai point.
Movements 9 ～ 10 are continuous.

【Hands】
Bring both fists to the hips.

【Feet】
Using the right foot as a pivot rotate counter-clockwise, and using Suri-Ashi pull the left foot to meet the right, with both feet directly facing the rear.

【Hands】
Position both fists on the hips (Back of both fists facing forward).

【Feet】
Heisokudachi.

【Note】
Move slowly, with the head, hands, and feet moving at the same speed.

【Hands】
Keep hands in the same position.

【Feet】
Bring the right knee up to the right hip.

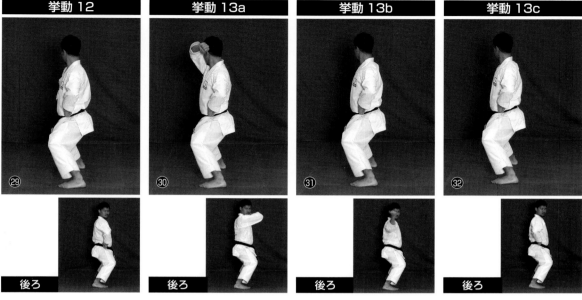

【Hands】
Keeping the hands in the same position, execute Right-Empi-Yoko-Uchi.

【Feet】
Rotate hips to the left and with the right foot stamp forward into kibadachi.

【Hands】
Moving the right fist up past the jaw to in front of the forehead, prepare for the next move.

【Feet】
Keep the same stance.

【Hands】
Snapping with the elbow, Right-Uraken-Tate-Mawashi-Uchi to the right side.

【Feet】
Keep the same stance.

【Hands】
Quickly bring the the right fist back to the right hip.

【Feet】
Keep the same stance.

◀右足で相手の膝に踏み込みながら、右猿臂で相手の突きを横に払う。さらに右裏拳で相手の上段（人中）を攻撃する。

While stamping with the right foot to the knee, deflect the opponent's punch with Empi-Barai. Then strike Right-Uraken to the opponent's philtrum (just below the nose).

途中	挙動 14	挙動 15a	挙動 15b
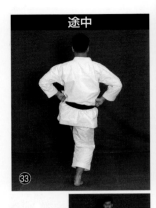 ㉝	 ㉞	 ㉟	 ㊱
後ろ	後ろ	後ろ	後ろ

【手の動作】
手の位置はそのまま

【足の動作】
腰の高さを変えずに、裏正面を向き、左膝を高くかい込む

【手の動作】
左猿臂（エンピ）横打ち
（手の位置はそのまま）

【足の動作】
左足一歩前に踏み込み、騎馬立ち

【手の動作】
左拳は顎前から額前へ、次の動作の準備

【足の動作】
立ち方はそのまま

【手の動作】
肘のスナップを効かせ左裏拳左側面縦回打ち

【足の動作】
立ち方はそのまま

【Hands】
Keep hands in the same position.

【Feet】
Without changing the stance height, face the rear and bring the left knee up to the left hip.

【Hands】
Left-Empi-Yoko-Uchi
(Keeping the hands in the same position).

【Feet】
Stamp the left foot forward into Kibadachi.

【Hands】
Moving the left fist up past the jaw to in front of the forehead, prepare for the next move.

【Feet】
Keep the same stance.

【Hands】
Snapping with the elbow, Left-Uraken-Tate-Mawashi-Uchi to the left side.

【Feet】
Keep the same stance.

挙動 12〜13c の解釈

◀裏拳の縦回し打ちのコースは、拳の位置からそのまま打つのではなく、あごの前から額前に持っていき、肘のスナップを効かせて上段（人中）を打つ。

Rather than striking directly from the starting position, the Uraken-Tate-Mawashi-Uchi should be brought up past in front of the jaw to in front of the forehead, then snapping at the elbow strike Jodan to the philtrum (just below the nose).

挙動 15c

【手の動作】
左拳を素早くもとの左腰に持っていく

【足の動作】
立ち方はそのまま

途中

【手の動作】
手の位置はそのまま

【足の動作】
腰の高さを変えずに、裏正面を向き右膝を高くかい込む

挙動 16

【手の動作】
両拳の位置はそのまま右猿臂（エンピ）横打ち

【足の動作】
右足一歩前に踏み込み、騎馬立ち

挙動 17a

【手の動作】
右拳は顎前から額前へ、次の動作の準備

【足の動作】
立ち方はそのまま

【Hands】
Quickly return the left fist to the left hip.

【Feet】
Keep the same stance.

【Hands】
Keep hands in the same position.

【Feet】
Without changing the stance height, face the rear and bring the right knee up to the right hip.

【Hands】
Keeping the hands in the same position, execute Right-Empi-Yoko-Uchi.

【Feet】
Stamp the right foot forward into Kibadachi.

【Hands】
Moving the right fist up past the jaw to in front of the forehead, prepare for the next move.

【Feet】
Keep the same stance.

挙動17b	挙動17c	途中	挙動18
 ㊶	 ㊷	 ㊸	 ㊹
後ろ	後ろ	後ろ 	後ろ 

【手の動作】
肘のスナップを効かせ右裏拳右側面縦回打ち

【足の動作】
立ち方はそのまま

【手の動作】
右拳を素早くもとの右腰に持っていく

【足の動作】
立ち方はそのまま

【手の動作】
右手を開き、ゆっくり前に出す。左拳は左脇腹にもっていき、次の動作の準備

【足の動作】
立ち方はそのまま

【手の動作】
左中段順突き

【足の動作】
左前屈立ち

【Hands】
Snapping with the elbow, Right-Uraken-Tate-Mawashi-Uchi to the right side.

【Feet】
Keep the same stance.

【Hands】
Quickly return the right fist to the right hip.

【Feet】
Keep the same stance.

【Hands】
Open the right hand and slowly extend it out in front. Prepare for the next move by readying the left fist on the left side of the body.

【Feet】
Keep the same stance.

【Hands】
Left-Chudan-Junzuki.

【Feet】
Left-Zenkutsudachi.

【手の動作】
手の位置はそのまま

【足の動作】
右足を引き寄せ、左足と同一線上に踵を並べる

【手の動作】
右拳突上げ（右拳甲上向き）、左猿臂後当て

【足の動作】
騎馬立ち

【手の動作】
左拳突上げ（左拳甲上向き）、右猿臂後当て

【足の動作】
騎馬立ちのまま、右側方へ寄り足をする。

【留意点】
気合いを入れる

【手の動作】
両拳を大腿部前にもっていく（両拳甲前向き）

【足の動作】
右足を半歩戻して八字立ち

【Hands】
Keep hands in the same position.

【Feet】
Pull the right foot up to alongside the left, so that the heels are on the same horizontal line.

【Hands】
Execute a Right-Tsukiage (back of the fist facing upwards)、and a Left-Empi-Ushiro-Ate.

【Feet】
Kibadachi.

【Hands】
Execute a Left-Tsukiage (back of the fist facing upwards)、and a Right-Empi-Ushiro-Ate.

【Feet】
Staying in Kibadachi、shift to the right using Yori-Ashi.

【Note】
Kiai point.

【Hands】
Move both fists to in front of the thighs(the back of both fists facing front).

【Feet】
Move the right foot half a step in to Hachijidachi.

◀後ろから抱きついてきたとき、素早く腰を落とすと同時に、左拳で相手の上段（顔面）を突き上げるとともに右猿臂で腹部を攻撃する。

When grabbed from behind, immediately drop the hips and at the same time strike both the opponent's face with Left-Tsukiage and the midsection with a Right-Empi.

【手の動作】
両手は開いて大腿部両側につけて伸ばす

※礼をする

【足の動作】
左足、右足の順に閉じて結び立ち

【Hands】
Open both hands and stretch the arms down to the sides of the thighs.

※ Bow (Rei).

【Feet】
In order, move left foot then right foot into Musubidachi.

平安四段
Heian Yondan
（27 挙動）

手の動作に下段交差受け、中段搔（か）き分け受け、裏拳縦回し打ち、足の動作に交差立ちが加わる。平安二段と同じように、ほとんどすべての基本技を含んでおり、変化に富んだ形なので技の緩急なども体得できる。特殊な使い方として膝当てをするため両拳を右膝両側に引きおろすなどの高度な技もある。演武線はほぼ「土」字形になる。

Hand techniques in Heian Yondan include Gedan-Kousa-Uke (low cross-handed block), Chudan-Kakiwake-Uke, and Uraken-Tate-Mawashi-Uchi (a vertical circular back-fist strike); the foot movement also introduces Kousadachi (crossed leg stance). Just like in Heian Nidan, almost all basic techniques are found in this kata. Because of this wide variety, you can better understand principles such as the pacing of these techniques. Special uses of Heian Yondan include becoming proficient in the advanced skill of pulling both hands down to either side of your right knee in order to strike your opponent with it. The 'footprint' movement line for this kata looks similar to the Japanese Kanji (character) for 'soil': '土'.

平安四段　挙動一覧

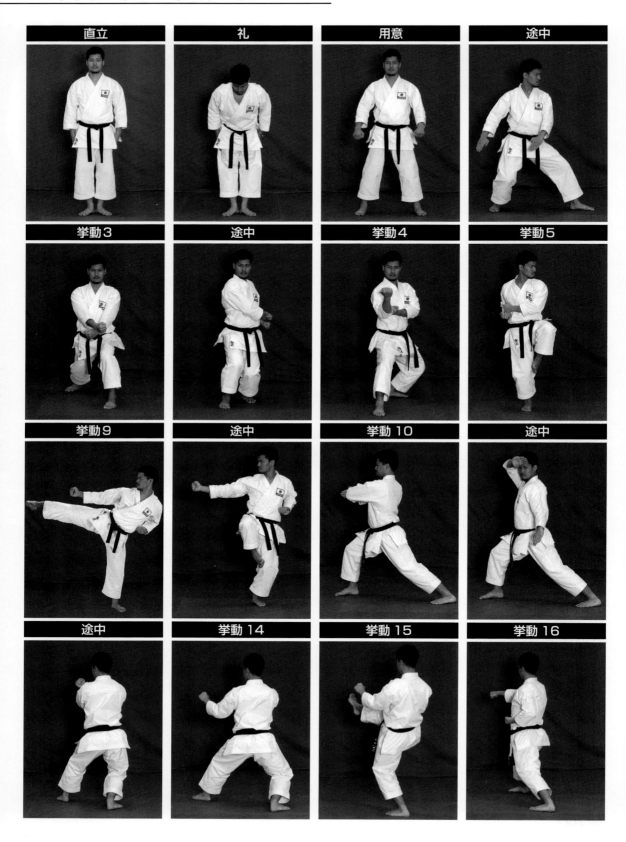

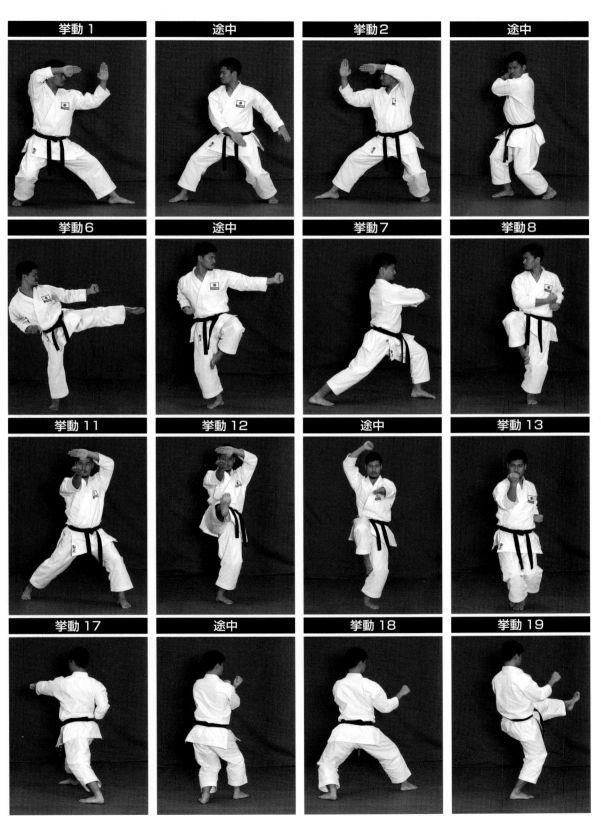

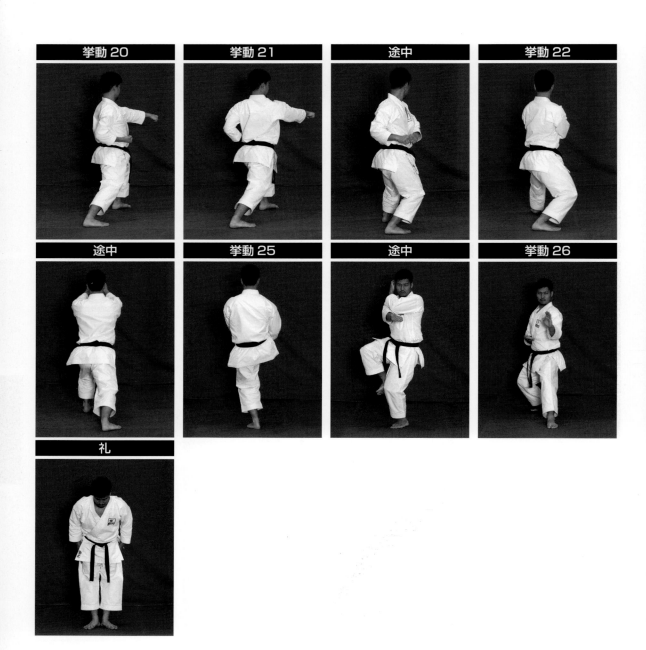

平安四段　各挙動解説

① 直立

② 礼

③ 用意

④ 途中

【手の動作】
両手は開いて大腿部両側につけて伸ばす

【足の動作】
結び立ち（左右とも正面に対して約30度）

※礼をする

【手の動作】
両拳を大腿部前にもっていく

【足の動作】
左足、右足の順に開いて八字立ち

【手の動作】
顔を左に向けるとともに、両拳を開く

【足の動作】
右脚を軸にして、ゆっくり左足をすり足で進める

【Hands】
Open both hands and stretch the arms down to the sides of the thighs.

【Feet】
Musubidachi (left and right feet are angled approximately 30 degrees from front).

※ Bow (Rei).

【Hands】
Move both fists to in front of the thighs.

【Feet】
In order, move left foot then right foot to Hachijidachi.

【Hands】
Look to the left and open both hands.

【Feet】
Pivoting on the Right foot, slowly move the left foot using Suri-Ashi.

64

挙動1	途中	挙動2	途中

⑤ ⑥ ⑦ ⑧

【手の動作】
ゆっくり左背腕左側面上段横受け、右前腕額前横構え（両掌甲後向）

【足の動作】
手足同時になるようにして右後屈立ち

【留意点】
手、足の動きを合わせ、ゆっくりと動かす

【手の動作】
両掌を左腰前に構える

【足の動作】
軸足を左脚に移す

【手の動作】
ゆっくり右背腕右側面上段横受け、左前腕額前横構え（両掌甲後向）

【足の動作】
手足同時になるようにして左後屈立ち

【留意点】
手、足の動きを合わせ、ゆっくりと動かす

【手の動作】
両掌を握り、右肩前で右拳を上、左拳を下にして交差させ、次の動作の準備

【足の動作】
右脚を軸に左足を正面にすり足で進める

【Hands】
Slowly execute a Left-Haiwan Jodan-Yoko-Uke to the left side, and hold the right forearm to in front of the forehead (the back of both hands facing the rear).

【Feet】
At the same time as the hand movement, move into Right-Kokutsudachi.

【Note】
The hands and feet should move at the same slow speed.

【Hands】
Position both fists in front of the left hip.

【Feet】
Transfer weight onto the left foot.

【Hands】
Slowly execute a Right-Haiwan Jodan-Yoko-Uke to the right side, and hold the left forearm to in front of the forehead (the back of both hands facing the rear).

【Feet】
At the same time as the hand movement, move into Left-Kokutsudachi.

【Note】
The hands and feet should move at the same slow speed.

【Hands】
Prepare for the next move by closing both hands and crossing them in front of the right shoulder, with the right fist above the left.

【Feet】
Pivoting on the right foot, move the left foot to the front using Suri-Ashi.

挙動3	途中	挙動4	挙動5
 ⑨	 ⑩	 ⑪	 ⑫

【手の動作】
両拳下段交差受け（両拳内向きで右手上）

【足の動作】
左前屈立ち

【手の動作】
両拳を左腰前へ、次の動作の準備

【足の動作】
右足を正面にすり足で進める

【手の動作】
右中段諸手受け（右肘内側に左拳の小指側を添える）

【足の動作】
左後屈立ち

【手の動作】
右拳の上に左拳を重ね、両拳右腰構え

【足の動作】
左足裏を右膝の横に抱え込みながら右脚立ち

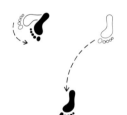   

【Hands】
With both fists, Gedan-Kousa-Uke (both fists facing inward, with the right hand on top).

【Feet】
Left-Zenkutsudachi.

【Hands】
Bring both fists to in front of the left hip and prepare for the next move.

【Feet】
Move the right foot towards the front using Suri-Ashi.

【Hands】
Right-Chudan-Morote-Uke (Align the little finger side of the left fist to the inside of the right elbow).

【Feet】
Left-Kokutsudachi.

【Hands】
Position both fists at the right hip, with the left fist laid on top of the right.

【Feet】
Stand on the right leg and hold the sole of the left foot against the inside of the right knee.

挙動6	途中	挙動7	挙動8
 ⑬	 ⑭	 ⑮	 ⑯

【手の動作】
左裏拳左側面上段横回打ち

【足の動作】
左中段横蹴上げ

【手の動作】
手の位置はそのまま

【足の動作】
蹴上げた左足を右膝まで寄せて、次の動作の準備

【手の動作】
右前猿臂（エンピ）

【足の動作】
左前屈立ち

【留意点】
挙動5〜7は続ける

【手の動作】
両拳左腰構え

【足の動作】
左足を半歩右に引きよせて、右足裏を左膝の横に抱え込みながら左脚立ち

 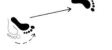 

【Hands】
Left-Uraken-Jodan-Yoko-Mawashi-Uchi to the left side.

【Feet】
Left-Chudan-Yoko-Keage.

【Hands】
Keep hands in the same position.

【Feet】
Return the left foot back to the right knee and prepare for the next move.

【Hands】
Right-Mae-Empi.

【Feet】
Left-Zenkutsudachi.

【Note】
Movements 5 〜 7 are continuous.

【Hands】
Position both fists on the left hip.

【Feet】
Pull the left foot half a step to the right, then standing on the left leg hold the sole of the right foot against the inside of the left knee.

挙動6〜7の解釈

◀裏拳で上段突きを受けると同時に、左足で横蹴上げをする。さらに裏拳を開き、相手の右手首を引きよせながら、相手の腹部を猿臂（エンピ）で攻撃する。

At the same time as blocking the Jodan-Tsuki with Uraken, execute a left side kick (Yoko-Keage). Then, open the Uraken and grab the opponent's right wrist, pulling it towards you, and strike Empi to the opponent's midsection.

挙動9	途中	挙動10	途中
⑰	⑱	⑲	⑳

【手の動作】
右裏拳右側面上段横回打ち

【足の動作】
右中段横蹴上げ

【手の動作】
手の位置はそのまま

【足の動作】
蹴上げた右足を膝横に戻し、次の動作の準備

【手の動作】
左前猿臂（エンピ）

【足の動作】
右前屈立ち

【留意点】
挙動8〜10は続ける

【手の動作】
右掌は額前に移すと同時に、左手刀で下段受け

【足の動作】
足の位置はそのまま

【Hands】
Right-Uraken-Jodan-Yoko-Mawashi-Uchi to the right side.

【Feet】
Right-Chudan-Yoko-Keage.

【Hands】
Keep hands in the same position.

【Feet】
Return the right foot back to the left knee and prepare for the next move.

【Hands】
Left-Mae-Empi.

【Feet】
Right-Zenkutsudachi.

【Note】
Movements 8 〜 10 are continuous.

【Hands】
Simultaneously move the open right hand to in front of the forehead and execute a Left-Shuto-Gedan-Uke.

【Feet】
Keep the same stance.

挙動10〜13の解釈

挙動11	挙動12	途中	挙動13

㉑	㉒	㉓	㉔

【手の動作】
右掌は額前から右へ大きく半円を描いて正面へ右手刀上段横回し打ち、左掌は下から回し額前へ左掌上段受け

【足の動作】
足の位置はそのままにして腰を左に回転させ、それに応じて両足を正面に向け左膝屈

【手の動作】
手の位置はそのまま

【足の動作】
右中段前蹴り、左脚立ち

【手の動作】
左手を前に出し（甲上向き）、右掌を握り顔の前を縦に回しながら、次の動作の準備

【足の動作】
蹴り足をかい込む

【手の動作】
右裏拳縦回し打ち、左拳左腰

【足の動作】
右足前交差立ち

【留意点】
気合いを入れる
一歩半飛び込む

【Hands】
From the forehead execute a Right-Shuto-Jodan-Yoko-Mawashi-Uchi by extending the right open hand to the front in a large semicircle. Bring the left hand up to the forehead, blocking Jodan-Uke with an open hand.

【Feet】
Keeping the same stance rotate the body to the left, allowing the force to turn both feet to face the front, with the left knee bent.

【Hands】
Keep hands in the same position.

【Feet】
Standing on the left leg, Right-Chudan-Maegeri.

【Hands】
Extend the left hand out in front (backhand facing upwards), close the right hand and rotate it up in front of the face, preparing for the next move.

【Feet】
Pull the kicking leg back in.

【Hands】
Right-Uraken-Tate-Mawashi-Uchi, pull the left fist to the left hip.

【Feet】
With the right foot in front, Kousadachi.

【Note】
Kiai point.
Jump one and a half steps forward.

◀相手の右中段蹴りを左手刀で下段受けして、右掌を額前から半円を描き相手の首を打つ。さらに右中段蹴りで攻撃しながら、相手の右順突きを左掌で押さえながら、右裏拳で上段（人中）を攻撃する。

Block the opponent's Chudangeri with Left-Shuto-Gedan-Uke, and with the right hand strike from the forehead in a semi-circular motion to the opponent's neck. Then, while kicking Right-Chudan-Keri, push down the opponent's Right-Junzuki with the left open hand and strike Right-Uraken to the philtrum (just below the nose).

挙動14　挙動15　挙動16

【手の動作】
両腕を胸前で交差させ、次の動作の準備

【足の動作】
右脚を軸に体を左に回転させ、左足を裏正面左斜め前にすり足でゆっくり移す

【手の動作】
両腕でゆっくり両拳中段掻き分け受け（両甲外斜上向き）

【足の動作】
手と動作を合わせ右後屈立ち

【留意点】
ゆっくり力を入れる

【手の動作】
手の位置はそのまま

【足の動作】
右中段前蹴り、左脚立ち

【手の動作】
右足をおろすと同時に右中段順突き、左拳左腰

【足の動作】
右前屈立ち

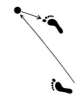

【Hands】
Prepare for the next move by crossing arms in front of the chest.

【Feet】
Using the right foot as a pivot slowly rotate the body counter-clockwise to face diagonally left towards the rear, and pull the left foot using Suri-Ashi.

【Hands】
Slowly uncross both arms into Chudan-Kakiwake-Uke (both backfists facing outwards and diagonally upwards).

【Feet】
Matching the movement timing of the hands, Right-Kokutsudachi.

【Note】
slowly put power into the movement.

【Hands】
Keep hands in the same position.

【Feet】
Standing on the left leg, Right-Chudan-Maegeri.

【Hands】
Punch Right-Chudan-Junzuki at the same time as putting the right foot down, and pull the left fist to the left hip.

【Feet】
Right-Zenkutsudachi.

挙動14〜17の解釈

挙動 17

【手の動作】
左拳中段逆突き

【足の動作】
足の位置はそのまま

【留意点】
挙動16〜17は続ける

【Hands】
 Left-Chudan-Gyakuzuki.

【Feet】
 Keep the same stance.

【Note】
Movements 16 〜 17 are continuous.

途中

【手の動作】
両腕を胸前で交差させ、次の動作の準備

【足の動作】
左脚を軸に体を裏正面右斜め前にすり足でゆっくり移す

【Hands】
Prepare for the next move by crossing arms in front of the chest.

【Feet】
Using the left foot as a pivot slowly rotate the body to face face diagonally right towards the rear, and pull the right foot using Suri-Ashi.

挙動 18

【手の動作】
両腕でゆっくり両拳中段掻き分け受け（両甲外斜上向き）

【足の動作】
手と動作を合わせ左後屈立ち

【留意点】
ゆっくり力を入れる

【Hands】
Slowly uncross both arms into Chudan-Kakiwake-Uke (both backfists facing outwards and diagonally upwards).

【Feet】
Matching the movement speed of the hands, Left-Kokutsudachi.

【Note】
slowly put power into the movement.

挙動 19

【手の動作】
手の位置はそのまま

【足の動作】
左中段前蹴り、右脚立ち

【Hands】
Keep hands in the same position.

【Feet】
Standing on the right leg, Left-Chudan-Maegeri.

◀相手が両手でつかんでくるところを、両手を内側に入れて掻き分けて前蹴りをする。続いて順突き逆突きで連続して攻撃をする。

After the opponent tries to grab both hands, move them to the inside, then force the opponent's arms apart and kick Maegeri. Continue by striking Junzuki then Guakuzuki in combination.

71

挙動20	挙動21	途中	挙動22
 ㉝	 ㉞	 ㉟	 ㊱
後ろ	後ろ	後ろ	後ろ

【手の動作】
左足をおろすと同時に左中段順突き、右拳右腰

【足の動作】
左前屈立ち

【手の動作】
右拳中段逆突き

【足の動作】
足の位置はそのまま

【留意点】
挙動20〜21は続ける

【手の動作】
両拳を右腰前に持っていき、次の動作の準備

【足の動作】
右脚を軸に左足を裏正面に移す

【手の動作】
左中段諸手受け（左肘内側に右拳の小指側を添える）

【足の動作】
右後屈立ち

【Hands】
Punch Left-Chudan-Junzuki at the same time as putting the left foot down, and pull the right fist to the right hip.

【Feet】
Left-Zenkutsudachi.

【Hands】
Right-Chudan-Gyakuzuki.

【Feet】
Keep the same stance.

【Note】
Movements 20 〜 21 are continuous.

【Hands】
Prepare for the next move by holding both fists in front of the right hip.

【Feet】
Pivoting on the right foot, move the left foot to face the rear.

【Hands】
Left-Chudan-Morote-Uke. (Align the little finger side of the right fist to the inside of the left elbow)

【Feet】
Right-Kokutsudachi.

途中 / 挙動23 / 途中 / 挙動24

後ろ / 後ろ / 後ろ / 後ろ

【手の動作】
両拳を左腰前に持っていき、次の動作の準備

【足の動作】
左脚を軸に右足を裏正面にすり足で進める

【手の動作】
右中段諸手受け

【足の動作】
左後屈立ち

【手の動作】
両拳を左腰前に持っていき、次の動作の準備

【足の動作】
右脚を軸に左足を裏正面にすり足で進める

【手の動作】
左中段諸手受け

【足の動作】
右後屈立ち

【Hands】
Prepare for the next move by holding both fists in front of the left hip.

【Feet】
Pivoting on the left foot, move the right foot towards the rear using Suri-Ashi.

【Hands】
Right-Chudan-Morote-Uke.

【Feet】
Left-Kokutsudachi.

【Hands】
Prepare for the next move by bringing both fists to in front of the left hip.

【Feet】
Pivoting on the right foot, move the left foot towards the rear using Suri-Ashi.

【Hands】
Left-Chudan-Morote-Uke.

【Feet】
Right-Kokutsudachi.

【手の動作】
両拳を開手して顔の前に出す

【足の動作】
そのままの位置で腰を切り左前屈

【手の動作】
両掌を握り右膝両側に引き下ろして右足のふくらはぎの横まで持っていき、右膝揚当て

【足の動作】
左脚立ち

【留意点】
気合いを入れる

【手の動作】
左掌は右肩上、右掌は甲を上にしてやや左ななめ下に出し、次の動作の準備

【足の動作】
左脚を軸に体を左に回転し、正面を向き振り向きながら右足をおろす

【手の動作】
左手刀中段受け

【足の動作】
右後屈立ち

【Hands】
Open both hands end extend out in front of the face.

【Feet】
Keeping the same feet position, twist the hips into Left-Zenkutsu.

【Hands】
Striking upwards with the right knee, close both fists and pull them down past both sides of the right knee to beside the calf.

【Feet】
Stand on the left leg.

【Note】
Kiai point.

【Hands】
Prepare for the next move by positioning the left open palm above the right shoulder. With the back of the hand facing up, extend the right open palm out in front, pointing slightly diagonally downward.

【Feet】
Using the left foot as a pivot rotate the body counter-clockwise, and while changing the direction of the body to directly face the front set down the right leg.

【Hands】
Left-Shuto-Chudan-Uke.

【Feet】
Right-Kokutsudachi.

◀両掌で相手の頭をつかみ引き寄せながら、膝で顔面を攻撃する。

Grab the opponent's head with both hands, and while pulling it down towards you strike with the knee to the face.

74

途中	挙動27	直れ	直立
 ㊺	 ㊻	 ㊼	 ㊽

【手の動作】
右掌は左肩上、左掌は甲を上にしてやや右ななめ下に出し、次の動作の準備

【足の動作】
左脚を軸に右足を前に進める

【手の動作】
右手刀中段受け

【足の動作】
左後屈立ち

【手の動作】
両拳を大腿部前にもっていく（両拳甲前向き）

【足の動作】
右足を引いて八字立ち

【手の動作】
両手は開いて大腿部両側につけて伸ばす

【足の動作】
左足、右足の順に閉じて結び立ち

【Hands】
Prepare for the next move by positioning the right open palm above the left shoulder. With the back of the hand facing up, extend the left open palm out in front, pointing slightly diagonally downward.

【Feet】
Pivoting on the left foot, move the right foot forward.

【Hands】
Right-Shuto-Chudan-Uke.

【Feet】
Left-Kokutsudachi.

【Hands】
Move both fists to in front of the thighs(the back of both fists facing front).

【Feet】
Pull the right foot into Hachijidachi.

【Hands】
Open both hands and stretch the arms down to the sides of the thighs.

【Feet】
In order, move left foot then right foot into Musubidachi.

※礼をする

※ Bow (Rei).

平安五段
Heian Godan
（23挙動）

手の動作に水流れの構え、両掌による上段交差受け、中段押え受け、騎馬立ちでの側面下段払いが加わる。飛び技など高度な技を体得する。三日月蹴り、飛び上がっての下段交差受け、手刀下段打込み、流し受けから上段外受けと下段受けを同時に素早く行うなど平安四段までに含まれていない多彩な技も体得できる。演武線は「T」字形となる。

The hand movements of Heian Godan include Mizunagare-no-Kamae (having the forearm tilt slightly downward from the elbow), Jodan-Kousa-Uke with open hands, Chudan-Osae-Uke ('pressing' block), as well as blocking Gedan-Barai to the side in Kibadachi. Advanced techniques, such as mid-air techniques, can be comprehended in this kata. You can also become proficient in many new skills which do not appear in the previous Heian kata, such as Mikazukigeri (crescent kick), jumping into Gedan-Kousa-Uke, Shuto-Gedan-Uchikomi, as well as going from a Nagashi-Uke (deflection block) to simultaneously and instantly blocking Jodan-Soto-Uke and Gedan-Uke. Like Heian Sandan, the 'footprint' movement line for this kata looks similar to a capital 'T'.

平安五段　挙動一覧

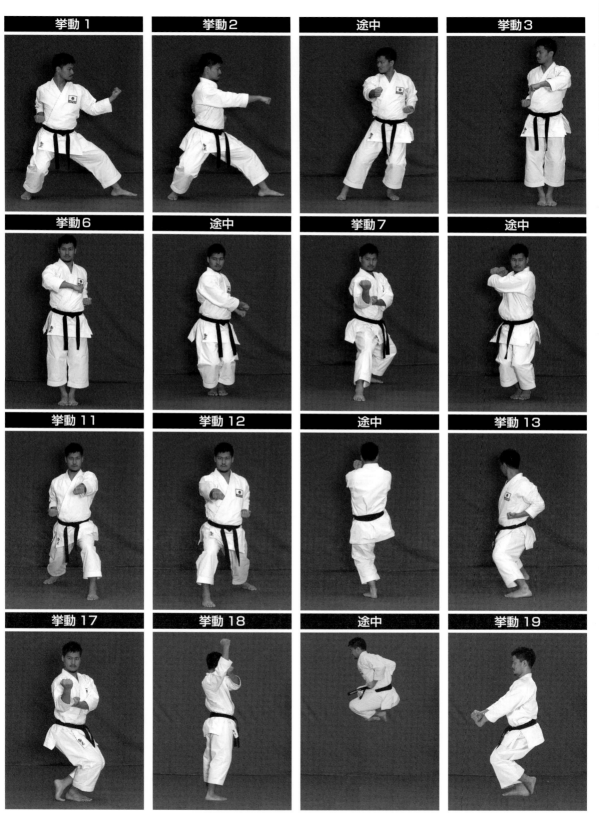

挙動21b	挙動22	途中	挙動23a

平安五段

平安五段　各挙動解説

 ① 直立
 ② 礼
 ③ 用意
 ④ 途中

【手の動作】
両手は開いて大腿部両側につけて伸ばす

【足の動作】
結び立ち（左右とも正面に対して約30度）

※礼をする

【手の動作】
両拳を大腿部前にもっていく

【足の動作】
左足、右足の順に開いて八字立ち

【手の動作】
右拳は左横に出し、左拳は右腰前に持っていき、次の動作の準備

【足の動作】
右脚を軸に左足をすり足で進める

【Hands】
Open both hands and stretch the arms down to the sides of the thighs.

【Feet】
Musubidachi (left and right feet are angled approximately 30 degrees from front).

※ Bow (Rei).

【Hands】
Move both fists to in front of the thighs.

【Feet】
In order, move left foot then right foot to Hachijidachi.

【Hands】
Prepare for the next move by extending the right fist to the left side, while at the same time moving the left fist to in front of the right hip.

【Feet】
Using the right foot as a pivot rotate to the left, move the left foot using Suri-Ashi.

挙動 1	挙動 2	途中	挙動 3

⑤	⑥	⑦	⑧

【手の動作】
左拳中段外受け

【足の動作】
右後屈立ち

【手の動作】
右拳中段逆突き

【足の動作】
立ち方はそのまま

【留意点】
挙動1～2は続ける

【手の動作】
ゆっくり顔を右に向けながら、同時に右拳を右腰に、左前腕は左拳が右脇前にくるようにして次の動作の準備

【足の動作】
手の動きと合わせて左足を正面に向けながら右足を引きつける

【手の動作】
左腕を水月前へ、左腕水流れの構え（甲上向）

【足の動作】
閉足立ち

【留意点】
顔、手、足の動きを合わせ、ゆっくりと動かす

【Hands】
Left-Chudan-Soto-Uke.

【Feet】
Right-Kokutsudachi.

【Hands】
Right-Chudan-Gyakuzuki.

【Feet】
Keep the same stance.

【Note】
Movements 1～2 are continuous.

【Hands】
Slowly turn the head to face right and simultaneously pull the right fist to the right hip and the left forearm and fist to the right side of the body, prepare for the next move.

【Feet】
While turning the left foot to face the front pull in the right foot, matching the movement of the hands.

【Hands】
Bring the right arm to in front of the sternum, in Mizunagare position (Forearm slightly pointing down, backfist facing upward).

【Feet】
Heisokudachi.

【Note】
The head, hands and feet should move at the same slow speed.

挙動1～2の解釈

◀相手の中段突きを左手で中段外受けし、左拳を開き相手の右手首を掴み引き寄せながら中段逆突きをする。

Block the opponent's Chudan-Tsuki with Left-Chudan-Soto-Uke, then opening the left hand grab and pull the opponent's right wrist, punching Chudan-Gyakuzuki at the same time.

83

【手の動作】
左拳は右横に出し、右拳は左腰前に持っていき、次の動作の準備

【足の動作】
左脚を軸に右足をすり足で進める

【手の動作】
右拳中段外受け

【足の動作】
左後屈立ち

【手の動作】
左拳中段逆突き

【足の動作】
立ち方はそのまま

【留意点】
挙動4〜5は続ける

【手の動作】
ゆっくり顔を正面に向けながら、同時に左拳を左腰に、右前腕は右拳が左脇前にくるようにして次の動作の準備

【足の動作】
手の動きと合わせて右足を正面に向けながら左足を引きつける

【Hands】
Prepare for the next move by extending the left fist to the right side, while at the same time moving the right fist to in front of the left hip.

【Feet】
Using the left foot as a pivot move the right foot using Suri-Ashi.

【Hands】
Right-Chudan-Soto-Uke.

【Feet】
Left-Kokutsudachi.

【Hands】
Left-Chudan-Gyakuzuki.

【Feet】
Keep the same stance.

【Note】
Movements 4〜5 are continuous.

【Hands】
Slowly turn the head to face the front and simultaneously pull the left fist to the left hip and the right forearm and fist to the left side of the body, prepare for the next move.

【Feet】
While turning the right foot to face the front pull in the left foot, matching the movement of the hands.

【手の動作】
右腕を水月前へ、右腕水流れの構え（甲上向）

【足の動作】
閉足立ち

【留意点】
顔、手、足の動きを合わせ、ゆっくりと動かす

【手の動作】
両拳を左腰前に持っていき、次の動作の準備

【足の動作】
左脚を軸に右足を正面にすり足で進める

【手の動作】
右中段諸手受け

【足の動作】
左後屈立ち

【手の動作】
右肩前で右拳を上、左拳を下にして交差させ、次の動作の準備

【足の動作】
右脚を軸に左足を正面にすり足で進める

【Hands】
Bring the right arm to in front of the sternum, in Mizunagare position (Forearm slightly pointing down, backfist facing upward).

【Feet】
Heisokudachi.

【Note】
The hands and feet should move together at the same slow speed.

【Hands】
Bring both fists to in front of the left hip and prepare for the next movement.

【Feet】
Pivoting on the left foot, move the right foot towards the front using Suri-Ashi.

【Hands】
Right-Chudan-Morote-Uke.

【Feet】
Left-Kokutsudachi.

【Hands】
Cross the hands in front of the right shoulder, with the right fist on top, and prepare for the next move.

【Feet】
Pivoting on the right foot, move the left foot towards the front using Suri-Ashi.

【手の動作】
両拳で下段交差受け（右手上）

【足の動作】
左前屈立ち

【手の動作】
両手首を交差したまま、胸前から額前へ両拳を開掌しながら次の動作の準備

【足の動作】
立ち方はそのまま

【手の動作】
両掌で上段交差受け

【足の動作】
立ち方はそのまま

【留意点】
挙動8〜9は続ける

【手の動作】
両手首をつけたまま、右掌の手首を捻り、両掌中段押え受け（右掌甲下向き、左掌甲上向き）

【足の動作】
立ち方はそのまま

【Hands】
With both fists execute Gedan-Kousa-Uke (right hand on top).

【Feet】
Left-Zenkutsudachi.

【Hands】
While keeping the hands crossed, move both fists past the front of the chest to in front of the forehead and prepare for the next move.

【Feet】
Keep the same stance.

【Hands】
With both hands execute Jodan-Kousa-Uke.

【Feet】
Keep the same stance.

【Note】
Movements 8 〜 9 are continuous.

【Hands】
Keeping the wrists connected, twist the right wrist and block Chudan-Osae-Uke with both hands (back of the right hand facing down, back of the left hand facing up).

【Feet】
Keep the same stance.

◀相手の中段前蹴りの足首を両拳ではさんで交差受けをする。

For Kousa-Uke, block the opponent's Chudan-Maegeri at the ankle, catching it between the two crossed fists.

挙動9〜12の解釈

【手の動作】
左拳中段突き

【足の動作】
立ち方はそのまま

【手の動作】
右拳中段順突き

【足の動作】
右前屈立ち

【留意点】
気合いを入れる
挙動11〜12は続ける

【手の動作】
右拳は左肩上に持っていき、左拳は伸ばし、次の動作の準備

【足の動作】
左脚を軸に、右足を後正面に踏み込む

【手の動作】
右拳右側面下段払い

【足の動作】
騎馬立ち

【Hands】
Right-Chudan-Tsuki.

【Feet】
Keep the same stance.

【Hands】
Right-Chudan-Junzuki.

【Feet】
Right-Zenkutsudachi.

【Note】
Kiai point.
Movements 11 〜 12 are continuous.

【Hands】
Bring the right fist to above the left shoulder, extend out the left hand and prepare for the next movement.

【Feet】
Pivoting on the left foot, bring up the right leg and stamp towards the rear.

【Hands】
With the right fist, block Gedan-Barai to the right side.

【Feet】
Kibadachi.

◀交差受けで相手の上段突きをはさみ、そのまま手首を返して、引き落とす。さらに突いてきた左拳を両掌でたたき落とし、中段突き、中段順突きをする

Trap the opponent's Jodan-Tsuki with Kousauke and, keeping the wrists positioned as they are, switch them over and pull down. Then, knock down the incoming left fist with both open hands, and strike Chudan-Tsuki, then Chudan-Junzuki.

87

|途中|挙動 14|挙動 15|挙動 16|

【手の動作】
顔を正面に向けながら右拳を左肩前に、左拳は開手して右脇腹へ、次の動作の準備

【足の動作】
立ち方はそのまま

【手の動作】
左掌を右肘下から横にゆっくり円を描いて、左掌左側面中段掛受け

【足の動作】
立ち方はそのまま

【留意点】
手はゆっくり動かす

【手の動作】
左脚を軸に腰を左に回しながら、右三日月蹴り

【足の動作】
左脚立ち

【手の動作】
右前猿臂（左掌に当てる）

【足の動作】
騎馬立ち

【Hands】
While the head is facing forward, bring the right fist to in front of the left shoulder, open the left hand and hold it at the right flank, and prepare for the next movement.

【Feet】
Keep the same stance.

【Hands】
Slowly circle the left open hand out from under the right elbow, and execute Chudan-Kake-Uke to the left hand side.

【Feet】
Keep the same stance.

【Note】
Move the hands slowly.

【Hands】
Pivoting on the left leg, execute Right-Mikazukigeri while rotating the hips counter-clockwise.

【Feet】
Stand on the left leg.

【Hands】
Right-Mae-Empi (strike the left palm).

【Feet】
Kibadachi.

挙動17	挙動18	途中	挙動19
 ㉙	 ㉚	 ㉛	 ㉜

横

【手の動作】
右中段諸手受け

【足の動作】
右脚に左足をよせて右足前交差立ち

【手の動作】
顔を後正面に向け右諸手後方突上げ

【足の動作】
レの字立ち（足幅は一足半）

【手の動作】
両拳を両腰に持っていく

【足の動作】
気合いとともに、左側方に膝をかい込んで飛ぶ

【留意点】
気合いを入れる

【手の動作】
両拳で下段交差受け

【足の動作】
右足前交差立ち

【Hands】
Right-Chudan-Morote-Uke.

【Feet】
Bringing the left foot towards the right foot, Kousadachi with the right foot in front.

【Hands】
With the head looking towards the rear, Right-Morote-Tsukiage in the opposite direction.

【Feet】
Renojidachi (stance width is approximately one and a half widths of your own foot).

【Hands】
Pull both fists to the hips.

【Feet】
At the same time as the Kiai, jump counter-clockwise while tucking up both knees.

【Note】
Kiai point.

【Hands】
With both fists execute Gedan-Kousa-Uke.

【Feet】
Kousadachi with the right foot forward.

挙動17～18の解釈

◀相手の左順突きを右中段諸手受けし、諸手で相手の顎を突き上げる。

Block the opponent's Left-Junzuki with Right-Chudan-Morote-Uke, then while turning the head to face another opponent in the other direction, strike the first opponent's jaw with Tsukiage, still held in Morote position.

	挙動20	途中	挙動21a

㉝	㉞	㉟	㊱

【手の動作】
両拳を左腰前に持っていき、次の動作の準備

【足の動作】
左脚を軸に右足を裏正面にすり足で進める

【手の動作】
右中段諸手受け

【足の動作】
右前屈立ち

【手の動作】
右掌を右肩上に、左掌を前に出し、次の動作の準備

【足の動作】
立ち方はそのまま

【手の動作】
右手刀下段打込み、左掌右肩上流し受け

【足の動作】
左脚前屈

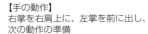

【Hands】
Bring both fists in front of the left hip and prepare for the next movement.

【Feet】
Pivoting on the left foot, move the right foot to the rear using Suri-Ashi.

【Hands】
Right-Chudan-Morote-Uke.

【Feet】
Right-Zenkutsudachi.

【Hands】
Move the right open hand to above the right shoulder, extend the left open hand out in front, and prepare for the next move.

【Feet】
Keep the same stance.

【Hands】
Right-Shuto-Gedan-Uchikomi, and block Nagashi-Uke with the left open hand above the right shoulder.

【Feet】
Left-Zenkutsu.

挙動21a〜21bの解釈

90

挙動21b	挙動22	途中	挙動23a

㊲	㊳	㊴	㊵

【手の動作】
右拳右側面上段外受け、左拳左側面下段受け

【足の動作】
右後屈立ち

【手の動作】
手はそのまま

【足の動作】
ゆっくり左足を右足に引き寄せ、閉足立ち

【留意点】
手、足の動きを合わせ、ゆっくりと動かす

【手の動作】
左掌は左肩上に、右掌は前に出し、次の動作の準備

【足の動作】
左脚を軸に体を左に回転させ正面を向き、次の動作の準備

【手の動作】
左手刀下段打込み、右掌左肩上流し受け

【足の動作】
右脚前屈

【Hands】
With the right fist block Jodan-Soto-Uke to the right side, and with the left fist block Gedan-Barai to the left side.

【Feet】
Right-Kokutsudachi.

【Hands】
Keep hands in the same position.

【Feet】
Slowly pull the left foot back to the right foot's position, Heisokudachi.

【Note】
The hands and feet should move at the same slow speed.

【Hands】
Move the left open hand to above the left shoulder, extend the right open hand out in front, and prepare for the next move.

【Feet】
Using the left foot as a pivot rotate the body counter-clockwise to face the front, preparing for the next move.

【Hands】
Left-Shuto-Gedan-Uchikomi, and block Nagashi-Uke with the right open hand above the left shoulder.

【Feet】
Right-Zenkutsu.

◀相手の右順突きを左掌で流し受けをするとともに、右手刀で下段打込みをする。打込んだ右手刀を引くと同時に左掌で相手の右手首をつかみ、相手の右足を左足で払う。

Deflect the opponent's Right-Junzuki with Nagashi-Uke executed with the left open hand, together with striking Right-Shuto-Gedan-Uchikomi. At the same time as pulling back the right hand, grab the opponent's right hand with your left and sweep the opponent's right leg with your left leg.

挙動23b	直れ	直立	礼
 ㊶	 ㊷	 ㊸	 ㊹

【手の動作】
左掌を握り下段から上段に、拳左側面上段外受け、右掌を握り、右拳左側面下段受け

【足の動作】
左後屈立ち

【手の動作】
両拳を大腿部前にもっていく（両拳甲前向き）

【足の動作】
右足を引いて八字立ち

【手の動作】
両手は開いて太腿部両側につけて伸ばす

【足の動作】
左足、右足の順に閉じて結び立ち

＊礼をする

 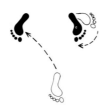 

【Hands】
Close both fists and pull the left up from Gedan to block Jodan-Soto-Uke to the left hand side, and block Right-Gedan-Uke to the right hand side.

【Feet】
Left-Kokutsudachi.

【Hands】
Move both fists to in front of the thighs(the back of both fists facing front).

【Feet】
Pull the right foot into Hachijidachi.

【Hands】
Open both hands and stretch the arms down to the sides of the thighs.

【Feet】
In order, move left foot then right foot into Musubidachi.

※ Bow (Rei).

鉄騎初段
Tekki Shodan
(29挙動)

鉄騎の形は初段から三段まであるが、もっとも代表的な形が鉄騎初段である。手の動作は鉤（かぎ）突き、背腕（はいわん）流し受けから上段裏突き、足の動作では騎馬立ちから波返しを行う技が加わる。この形では騎馬立ちが重要なポイントとなるので、騎馬立ちを崩さないで上体の動きをつくることを体得する。演武線は「一」字形で左右に移動する形である。

Although there are actually three Tekki Kata, Tekki Shodan is the most representative of the series. Hand techniques include Kagizuki (Hook punch), striking Jodan-Urazuki from Haiwan-Nagashi-Uke, while the foot movements include Namikaeshi (sweeping the leg upwards from the knee) from Kibadachi. As this kata puts great importance on Kibadachi, it teaches the proficiency of not upsetting the balance of Kibadachi while moving the upper body. Tekki Shodan's 'footprint' movement line is just like a hyphen, '一', as it only has movements to the left and right.

鉄騎初段　挙動一覧

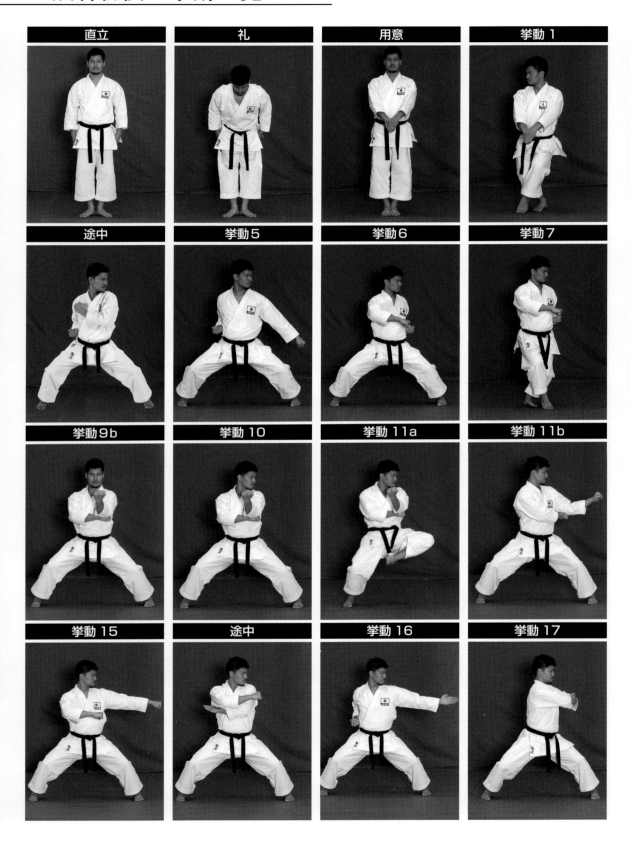

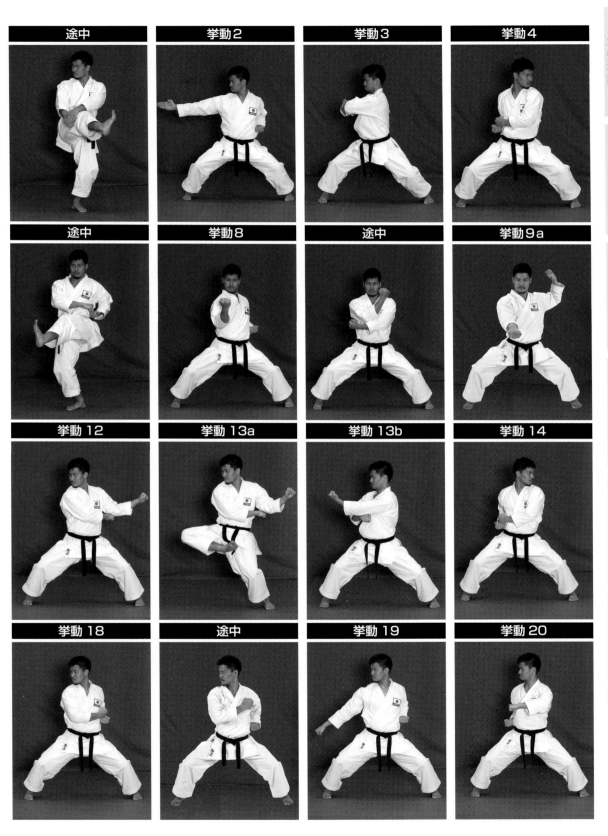

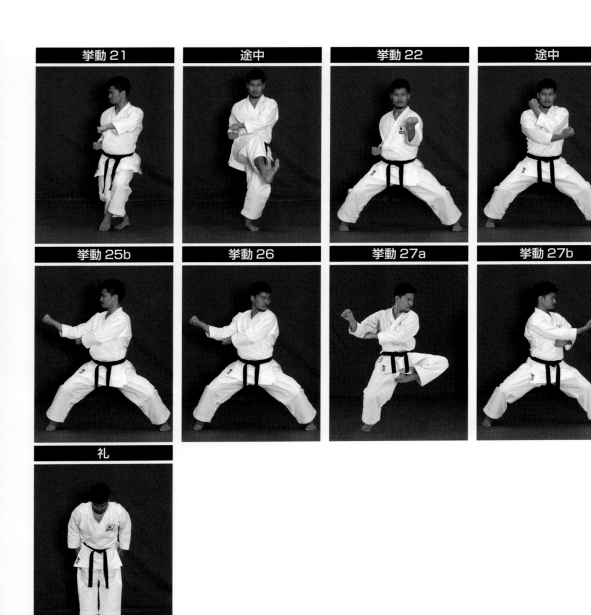

鉄騎初段　各挙動解説

直立	礼	用意	挙動 1

①	②	③	④

【手の動作】
両手は開いて大腿部両側につけて伸ばす

【足の動作】
結び立ち（左右とも正面に対して約30度）

※礼をする

【手の動作】
右掌の上に左掌を重ね、下腹部前に両掌を出す

【足の動作】
結び立から閉足立ちになる

【手の動作】
手はそのままにして、顔を右に向ける

【足の動作】
腰を落として、左足を右足に交差させる

【Hands】
Open both hands and stretch the arms down to the sides of the thighs.

【Feet】
Musubidachi (left and right feet are angled approximately 30 degrees from front).

※ Bow (Rei).

【Hands】
Rest the left palm on top of the right, and extend out in front of the lower abdomen.

【Feet】
Close feet from Musubidachi into Heisokudachi.

【Hands】
Keep hands in the same position, turning the head to face right.

【Feet】
Lowering the waist, cross the left foot over the right.

途中	挙動2	挙動3	挙動4
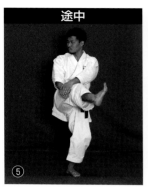 ⑤	 ⑥	 ⑦	 ⑧

【手の動作】
手の位置はそのまま

【足の動作】
左足をそのままにして、右足は左膝の後ろから膝を上げかい込んで、次の動作の準備

【手の動作】
左拳を左腰に引くと同時に右掌を胸前から回し、右掌右側面中段掛受け

【足の動作】
右足を右に踏み込み、騎馬立ち

【手の動作】
左前猿臂（エンピ）
（右掌に当てる）

【足の動作】
下半身をくずさず、足の位置はそのまま

【手の動作】
顔を左に向け、両拳右腰構え（左拳を甲前向きにして右拳の上に、右拳は甲下向き）

【足の動作】
立ち方はそのまま

【Hands】
Keep hands in the same position.

【Feet】
Keeping the left foot in the same position, bring the right foot from behind the left knee, bring up the right knee, and prepare for the next move.

【Hands】
At the same time as pulling the left fist to the left hip, circle the right open hand out from in front of the chest and execute Chudan-Kake-Uke to the right side.

【Feet】
Stamp into Kibadachi with the right foot, to the right side.

【Hands】
Left-Mae-Empi
(Strike the right palm).

【Feet】
Keep the same stance, without upsetting the balance of the lower half of the body.

【Hands】
Turn the head to face left and position both fists by the right hip (Left on top and backfist facing front, right underneath and backfist facing down).

【Feet】
Keep the same stance.

◀相手の中段突きを右掌で中段掛受けをし、さらに相手の左手首をつかみ、猿臂で攻撃する。

Block the opponent's Chudan-Tsuki with Kake-Uke, then grab the wrist and attack with an elbow (Empi) strike.

挙動2～3の解釈

【手の動作】
左拳を右胸前に持っていき、次の動作の準備

【足の動作】
立ち方はそのまま

【手の動作】
左下段払い

【足の動作】
立ち方はそのまま

【手の動作】
右腕は肘から先を曲げ水平に構えて、右拳鉤（かぎ）突き
左拳は左腰

【足の動作】
立ち方はそのまま

【手の動作】
手はそのまま

【足の動作】
左足はそのままにして、右足をゆっくり寄せて、右足前交差立ち

【留意点】
ゆっくり足を運ぶ

【Hands】
Bring the left fist in front of the right side of the chest, prepare for the next move.

【Feet】
Keep the same stance.

【Hands】
Left-Gedan-Barai

【Feet】
Keep the same stance.

【Hands】
Bending from the elbow and positioned horizontally, Right-Kagizuki (hook punch).
Pull the left fist to the left hip.

【Feet】
Keep the same stance.

【Hands】
Keep hands in the same position.

【Feet】
Keeping the left foot in the same position, Right foot forward Kousadachi.

【Note】
Advance slowly.

◀相手の右中段蹴りを左手で下段払いして、中段（腹部）を鉤（かぎ）突きで攻撃する

Block the opponent's Chudan-Keri with Gedan-Barai, then attack to the midsection (Chudan) with a hook punch (Kagizuki).

【手の動作】
顔を正面に向け、右肘の位置を変えないで、次の動作の準備

【足の動作】
右足はそのままにして、左足は右膝の後ろから膝をかい込んで、次の動作の準備

【手の動作】
右中段外受け

【足の動作】
左足を踏みこんで、騎馬立ち

【手の動作】
左拳は右肘の下に、右拳は左肩前に同時に持っていき、次の動作の準備

【足の動作】
立ち方はそのまま

【手の動作】
左背腕上段流し受け、右下段受け（甲上）

【足の動作】
立ち方はそのまま

【Hands】
Without changing the position of the right elbow turn the head to face forward and prepare for the next move.

【Feet】
Keeping the right foot in the same position, Bring the left foot from behind the right knee, bring up the left knee.

【Hands】
Right-Chudan-Soto-Uke.

【Feet】
Stamp the left foot down into Kibadachi.

【Hands】
Simultaneously bring the left fist to under the right elbow and the right fist to in front of the left shoulder, prepare for the next move.

【Feet】
Keep the same stance.

【Hands】
Execute Jodan-Nagashi-Uke with the outside of the left arm (Backfist facing out to the side), and Right-Gedan-Uke (backfist facing upward).

【Feet】
Keep the same stance.

挙動9b	挙動10	挙動11a	挙動11b

⑰	⑱	⑲	⑳

【手の動作】
左拳上段裏突きと同時に右拳を左肘の下に持っていく

【足の動作】
立ち方はそのまま

【手の動作】
顔だけ左を向き、手はそのまま

【足の動作】
立ち方はそのまま

【手の動作】
手の位置はそのまま

【足の動作】
右足はそのままにして、腰の位置を変えないで、左足波返し

【手の動作】
上体だけを左にひねり、左腕左側面中段受け

【足の動作】
騎馬立ち

【Hands】
At the same time as executing Left-Jodan-Urazuki bring the right fist to under the left elbow.

【Feet】
Keep the same stance.

【Hands】
Keep hands in the same position, turning only the head to face left.

【Feet】
Keep the same stance.

【Hands】
Keep hands in the same position.

【Feet】
Keeping the right foot in the same position. Without changing the position of the hips, sweep up the left leg (Namigaeshi).

【Hands】
Twisting only the upper body to the left, with the left arm block Chudan-Uke to the left hand side

【Feet】
Kibadachi.

挙動 12	挙動 13a	挙動 13b	挙動 14

【手の動作】
顔だけ右に向け、手はそのまま

【足の動作】
立ち方はそのまま

【手の動作】
手はそのまま

【足の動作】
左足はそのままにして、腰の位置を変えないで、右足波返し

【手の動作】
左拳を肘からひねり、左腕右側面中段受け

【足の動作】
騎馬立ち

【手の動作】
顔を左に向け、両拳を右腰に引きつける。手の位置は右拳（甲下）の上に左拳（甲前）

【足の動作】
立ち方はそのまま

【Hands】
Keep hands in the same position, turning only the head to face right.

【Feet】
Keep the same stance.

【Hands】
Keep hands in the same position.

【Feet】
Keeping the left foot in the same position. Without changing the position of the hips, sweep up the right leg (Namigaeshi).

【Hands】
Twisting the left fist from the elbow, with the left arm execute Chudan-Uke to the right hand side.

【Feet】
Kibadachi.

【Hands】
At the same time as turning the head to face left, pull both fists to the right hip, with the left fist (backfist facing forward) on top of the right (backfist facing down).

【Feet】
Keep the same stance.

挙動 15	途中	挙動 16	挙動 17

㉕	㉖	㉗	㉘

【手の動作】
両拳同時に左を突く。左側面中段突き、右拳は中段鉤（かぎ）突き

【足の動作】
立ち方はそのまま

【留意点】
気合いを入れる

【手の動作】
右拳を左肩前へ左掌を右脇腹に持っていき次の動作の準備

【足の動作】
立ち方はそのまま

【手の動作】
左掌は左側面中段掛受け、右拳右腰

【足の動作】
立ち方はそのまま

【留意点】
手はゆっくり動かす

【手の動作】
右前猿臂（エンピ）
（左掌に当てる）

【足の動作】
下半身を崩さず、立ち方はそのまま

【Hands】
Strike with both fists to the left side simultaneously; Left-Chudan-Tsuki with the left fist, and Chudan-Kagizuki (hook punch) with the right fist.

【Feet】
Keep the same stance.

【Note】
Kiai point.

【Hands】
Bring the right fist to in front of the left shoulder, the left open hand to the right flank, and prepare for the next movement.

【Feet】
Keep the same stance.

【Hands】
Execute Chudan-Kake-Uke with the left open hand to the left hand side, and pull the right fist to the right hip

【Feet】
Keep the same stance.

【Note】
Move the hands slowly.

【Hands】
Right-Mae-Empi
(strike the left palm).

【Feet】
Keep the same stance, without upsetting the balance of the lower half of the body.

挙動18	途中	挙動19	挙動20
 ㉙	 ㉚	 ㉛	 ㉜

【手の動作】
顔を右に向けると同時に、両拳左腰構え。右拳は左拳の上に重ねる

【足の動作】
立ち方はそのまま

【手の動作】
右拳を左胸前に持っていき、次の動作の準備

【足の動作】
立ち方はそのまま

【手の動作】
右下段払い

【足の動作】
立ち方はそのまま

【手の動作】
左腕は肘から先を曲げ水平に構えて、左拳鉤（かぎ）突き
右拳は右腰

【足の動作】
立ち方はそのまま

【Hands】
Turn the head to face right and position both fists by the left hip (Right fist on top).

【Feet】
Keep the same stance.

【Hands】
Bring the right fist in front of the left side of the chest, prepare for the next move.

【Feet】
Keep the same stance.

【Hands】
Right-Gedan-Barai.

【Feet】
Keep the same stance.

【Hands】
Bending from the elbow and positioned horizontally, Left-Kagizuki (hook punch).
Pull the right fist to the right hip.

【Feet】
Keep the same stance.

| 挙動21 | 途中 | 挙動22 | 途中 |

【手の動作】
手はそのまま

【足の動作】
右足はそのままにして、左足を寄せて、左足前交差立ち

【留意点】
ゆっくり足を運ぶ

【手の動作】
顔を正面に向け、左肘の位置を変えないで、次の動作の準備

【足の動作】
左足をそのままにして、右足は左膝の後ろから膝をかい込んで、次の動作の準備

【手の動作】
左中段外受け

【足の動作】
騎馬立ち

【手の動作】
右拳を左肘の下に、左拳は右肩前に同時に持っていき、次の動作の準備

【足の動作】
立ち方はそのまま

【Hands】
Keep hands in the same position.

【Feet】
Keeping the right foot in the same position, Left foot forward Kousadachi.

【Note】
Advance slowly.

【Hands】
Without changing the position of the left elbow turn the head to face forward and prepare for the next move.

【Feet】
Keeping the left foot in the same position, bring the right foot from behind the left knee, bring up the right knee, and prepare for the next move.

【Hands】
Left-Chudan-Soto-Uke.

【Feet】
Kibadachi.

【Hands】
Simultaneously bring the right fist to under the left elbow and the left fist to in front of the right shoulder, prepare for the next move.

【Feet】
Keep the same stance.

挙動 23a	挙動 23b	挙動 24	挙動 25a

【手の動作】
右背腕上段流し受け、左下段受け（甲上）

【足の動作】
立ち方はそのまま

【手の動作】
右拳上段裏突きと同時に左拳を右肘の下に持っていく

【足の動作】
立ち方はそのまま

【手の動作】
顔だけ右に向け、手はそのまま

【足の動作】
立ち方はそのまま

【手の動作】
手はそのまま

【足の動作】
左足はそのままにして、腰の位置を変えないで、右足波返し

【Hands】
Execute Jodan-Nagashi-Uke with the outside of the right arm (Backfist facing out to the side), and Left-Gedan-Uke (backfist facing upward).

【Feet】
Keep the same stance.

【Hands】
At the same time as executing Right-Jodan-Urazuki bring the left fist to under the right elbow.

【Feet】
Keep the same stance.

【Hands】
Keep hands in the same position, turning only the head to face right.

【Feet】
Keep the same stance.

【Hands】
Keep hands in the same position.

【Feet】
Keeping the left foot in the same position. Without changing the position of the hips, sweep up the right leg (Namigaeshi).

挙動 22～23b の解釈

◀右中段突きを左中段外受けし、さらに相手の左上段逆突きに対して流し受けを行い、右拳上段裏突きで上段（人中）を攻撃する。

Block the opponent's Right-Chudan-Tsuki with Left-Chudan-Soto-Uke, then execute Right-Nagashi-Uke against the Left-Jodan-Gyakuzuki, and counter with a Right-Jodan-Urazuki to the philtrum (just below the nose).

【手の動作】
上体だけを右にひねり、右腕右側面中段受け

【足の動作】
騎馬立ち

【手の動作】
顔だけ左を向き、手はそのまま

【足の動作】
立ち方はそのまま

【手の動作】
手はそのまま

【足の動作】
右足をそのままにして、腰の位置を変えないで、左足波返し

【手の動作】
右拳を肘からひねり、右腕左側面中段受け

【足の動作】
騎馬立ち

【手の動作】
Twisting only the upper body to the right, with the right arm block Chudan-Uke to the right hand side.

【Feet】
Kibadachi.

【Hands】
Keep hands in the same position, turning only the head to face left.

【Feet】
Keep the same stance.

【Hands】
Keep hands in the same position.

【Feet】
Keeping the right foot in the same position. Without changing the position of the hips, sweep up the left leg (Namigaeshi).

【Hands】
Twisting the right fist from the elbow, with the right arm execute Chudan-Uke to the left hand side.

【Feet】
Kibadachi.

108

挙動28	挙動29	直れ	直立

㊺	㊻	㊼	㊽

【手の動作】
顔を右に向けると同時に、両拳左腰構え。右拳は左拳の上に重ねる

【足の動作】
立ち方はそのまま

【手の動作】
両拳同時に右を突く。右側面中段突き、左拳は中段鉤(かぎ)突き

【足の動作】
立ち方はそのまま

【留意点】
気合いを入れる

【手の動作】
両拳を開手し右掌の上に左掌を重ね、下腹部前に両掌を出す

【足の動作】
右足を引いて閉足立ち

【手の動作】
両手は開いて大腿部両側につけて伸ばす

【足の動作】
結び立ち

【Hands】
At the same time as turning the head to face right pull both fists to the left hip, with the right fist on top of the left fist.

【Feet】
Keep the same stance.

【Hands】
Strike with both fists to the right side simultaneously; Right-Chudan-Tsuki with the right fist, and Chudan-Kagizuki (hook punch) with the left fist.

【Feet】
Keep the same stance.

【Note】
Kiai point.

【Hands】
Open both fists, rest the left palm on top of the right, and extend out in front of the lower abdomen.

【Feet】
Pull the right foot into Heisokudachi.

【Hancs】
Open both hands and stretch the arms down to the sides of the thighs.

【Feet】
Musubidachi.

※礼をする

※ Bow (Rei).

平安初段

平安二段

平安三段

平安四段

平安五段

鉄騎初段

監修

■（一財）全日本空手道松涛館　中央技術委員会　（＊印は基本形制定委員）

　＊津山捷泰　　Tsuyama Katsuhiro
　　澁谷　孝　　Shibuya Takashi
　＊阪梨　學　　Sakanashi Manabu
　＊香川政夫　　Kagawa Masao
　　西谷　賢　　Nishitani Satoshi
　　香川政義　　Kagawa Masayoshi
　　永木　満　　Nagaki Mitsuru
　　山川和忠　　Yamakawa Kazutada

■演武協力
　　在本幸司　　Arimoto Koji
　　西原啓太　　Nishihara Keita

松涛館流空手道形教範全集　基本形　平安初段～五段・鉄騎初段

2016年4月28日　第1版第1刷発行
2018年12月15日　第1版第2刷発行

編集　　一般財団法人全日本空手道松涛館　中央技術委員会
編者　　一般財団法人全日本空手道松涛館
発行　　株式会社チャンプ
　　　　〒166-0003　東京都杉並区高円寺南4-19-3 総和第二ビル
　　　　電話：03-3315-3190（営業部）

©ALL Japan Karatedo Shotokan 2016
Printed in Japan　印刷：シナノ印刷株式会社

定価はカバーに表示してあります。
乱丁・落丁本は、ご面倒ですが(株)チャンプ宛にご送付ください。送料小社負担にてお取り替えいたします。

ISBN978-4-86344-014-2